Mediterranean Air Fryer Cookbook for Weight Loss

1500 Days of Mouthwatering, Healthy, and Easy-to-Make Mediterranean Diet Recipes for Air Fryer Cooking. 30-Day Meal Plan Included

Kathleen H. Jensen

Copyright © 2023 by Kathleen H. Jensen.

All rights reserved. No part of this book may be used or reproduced in any form whatsoever without written permission except in the case of brief quotations in critical articles or reviews.

Printed in the United States of America.

CONTENTS

Introduction 1
   The Mediterranean Diet and the Air Fryer 1
Chapter 1 2
Chapter 2 4
SALADS 6
   Greek Quinoa Salad with Feta and Kalamata Olives 6
   Watermelon and Mint Salad with Feta 7
   Mediterranean Tuna and White Bean Salad 8
   Grilled Halloumi Salad with Fig Vinaigrette 9
   Mediterranean Watercress Salad with Pomegranate and Pistachios 10
   Roasted Beet and Quinoa Salad with Citrus Dressing 11
   Tabbouleh Salad with Cauliflower Rice 12
   Zucchini Ribbon Salad with Basil Pesto 13
   Radicchio and Blood Orange Salad with Toasted Pine Nuts 14
   Arugula and Roasted Grape Salad with Balsamic Vinaigrette 15
   Chickpea and Spinach Salad with Lemon-Tahini Dressing 15
   Roasted Fennel and Orange Salad with Toasted Hazelnuts 16
   Mediterranean Cucumber Ribbon Salad with Dill Yogurt Dressing ... 17
   Grilled Artichoke and Asparagus Salad with Lemon Herb Vinaigrette 18
   Roasted Carrot and Chickpea Salad with Cumin-Lemon Dressing ... 19
   Italian Caprese Salad with Avocado and Balsamic Glaze 21
   Greek Tuna and White Bean Salad with Dill 21
   Moroccan Spiced Cauliflower Salad with Tahini 22
   Mediterranean Watermelon Radish and Mint Salad 24
SOUPS 25
   Spicy Moroccan Lentil Soup 25
   Lemon Chicken Orzo Soup with Spinach 26
   Greek Avgolemono Soup with Shrimp 27

Roasted Tomato and Basil Soup with White Beans 28

Tuscan Ribollita Soup with Kale 29

Spanish Gazpacho with Avocado Salsa 30

Mediterranean Lentil and Spinach Soup 31

Roasted Eggplant and Tomato Soup 32

Greek Lemon Chickpea Soup 33

Italian White Bean and Kale Soup with Turkey Sausage 34

Tomato and Basil Quinoa Soup 36

Lebanese Red Lentil and Spinach Soup 37

Greek Lemon Rice Soup with Kale 38

Spanish White Bean and Garlic Soup 39

Moroccan Chickpea and Spinach Stew 40

Italian Minestrone Soup with Cannellini Beans 41

Mediterranean Lentil and Swiss Chard Soup 42

Spanish Chilled Almond and Garlic Soup (Ajo Blanco) 43

Greek Lemon Orzo Soup with Spinach and Chicken 44

Moroccan Harira Soup with Quinoa 45

SEAFOOD 47

Harissa Spiced Grilled Swordfish 47

Moroccan Baked Fish with Preserved Lemon and Olives 48

Garlic and Herb Shrimp Skewers 49

Greek-style Stuffed Calamari 50

Baked Cod with Mediterranean Tomato Sauce 50

Baked Lemon Herb Haddock 51

Moroccan Chermoula Grilled Prawns 52

Greek Stuffed Sole with Spinach and Feta 53

Sardine and Olive Tapenade Stuffed Bell Peppers 54

Tuscan-style Clam and Cannellini Bean Stew 55

Lemon Dill Baked Salmon with Asparagus 56

Spanish Grilled Mackerel with Romesco Sauce 57

Italian Stuffed Calamari with Spinach and Pine Nuts 58
Greek Baked Red Snapper with Mediterranean Salsa 59
Harissa Shrimp and Zucchini Noodles 60
Grilled Swordfish with Italian Salsa Verde 61
Spanish Baked Hake with Tomato and Bell Pepper Sauce 62
Lemon Herb Stuffed Trout with Almonds 63
Greek-style Seafood Paella 64
Moroccan Spiced Scallops with Roasted Red Pepper Sauce 66

POULTRY 68
Mediterranean Chicken Shawarma 68
Lemon Oregano Turkey Meatballs 69
Moroccan Spiced Chicken Tagine 70
Grilled Harissa Chicken Thighs 71
Spinach and Feta Stuffed Chicken Breast 72
Lemon Rosemary Grilled Turkey Breast 73
Mediterranean Chicken and Artichoke Skewers 74
Moroccan Chicken with Apricots and Almonds 75
Greek Lemon Garlic Chicken with Green Beans 76
Harissa Roasted Quail with Mint Yogurt Sauce 77
Italian Herb Roasted Turkey Cutlets 78
Greek Lemon Rosemary Chicken Thighs 79
Moroccan Chicken and Olive Tagine 80
Lemon Garlic Turkey and Vegetable Skewers 82
Tuscan Herb Stuffed Quail 83
Italian Herbed Turkey Meatloaf with Roasted Vegetables 84
Lemon Rosemary Chicken and Quinoa Bowls 85
Greek Lemon Garlic Turkey Cutlets with Tzatziki 87
Moroccan Spiced Chicken Skewers with Yogurt-Harissa Dip 88
Tuscan-style Turkey and White Bean Soup 89

VEGETARIAN AND VEGAN 92

Eggplant and Zucchini Moussaka 92

Vegan Mediterranean Stuffed Bell Peppers... 93

Spinach and Chickpea Curry 94

Mediterranean Roasted Vegetable Platter 96

Cilantro and Lemon Couscous with Dried Fruits and Nuts 97

Vegan Eggplant Parmesan with Spaghetti Squash... 98

Spanakopita Stuffed Portobello Mushrooms 99

Mediterranean Roasted Veggie Tacos with Tahini Sauce 100

Vegan Moroccan Lentil Stew.. 101

Artichoke and Sun-Dried Tomato Stuffed Peppers... 103

Mediterranean Stuffed Bell Peppers with Quinoa and Chickpeas................ 104

Vegan Greek Spinach and Rice Stuffed Tomatoes 105

Moroccan Chickpea and Vegetable Tagine 106

Eggplant and Lentil Moussaka 107

Vegan Italian Artichoke and Spinach Lasagna 109

Italian Eggplant and Zucchini Ratatouille..111

Greek Vegan Spanakopita with Tofu and Spinach 112

Moroccan Chickpea and Eggplant Tagine 113

Mediterranean Stuffed Acorn Squash with Bulgur 114

Vegan Italian Pasta Primavera with Lemon Garlic Sauce 115

PASTA AND GRAINS...117

Greek Spinach and Feta Stuffed Shells...117

Lebanese Lentil and Rice Pilaf 118

Mediterranean Farro Risotto with Roasted Tomatoes 120

Saffron-infused Moroccan Couscous 121

Lemon Garlic Shrimp and Asparagus Orzo 123

Moroccan Chickpea and Date Tagliatelle..124

Italian Farro and Roasted Vegetable Bowl..125

Greek Tzatziki Pasta Salad with Cucumber and Dill...127

Spinach and Ricotta Stuffed Shells with Tomato Sauce 128

Lemon Garlic Spaghetti with Roasted Cherry Tomatoes 129

Moroccan Spiced Couscous with Roasted Vegetables 131

Italian Brown Rice Risotto with Wild Mushrooms 132

Greek Orzo and Tomato Pilaf 134

Spinach and Ricotta Stuffed Pasta Shells with Marinara 135

Lemon Artichoke Linguine with Arugula and Walnuts 137

Greek-style Orzo Risotto with Sundried Tomatoes 138

Moroccan Couscous Pilaf with Apricots and Almonds 140

Mediterranean Spaghetti Squash with Roasted Red Pepper Sauce ... 141

LEGUMES AND BEANS 143

Spanish White Bean and Chorizo Stew 143

Italian-Style Lentil Salad with Sun-Dried Tomatoes 144

Greek Gigantes Plaki (Baked Giant Beans) 145

Chickpea and Artichoke Tagine 146

Tuscan White Bean and Rosemary Hummus 147

Lebanese Mujadara with Quinoa 148

Italian Cannellini Bean and Escarole Soup 148

Harissa Spiced Lentil Tacos 149

Greek-Style Butter Beans with Tomato and Dill 150

Italian White Bean and Escarole Salad with Lemon-Dijon Dressing ... 151

Spanish Chickpea and Chorizo Stew 152

Mediterranean Lentil and Eggplant Casserole 153

Harissa Spiced Chickpea and Spinach Saute 154

Greek-Style Gigantes Beans with Tomato and Parsley 155

Italian Lentil and Mushroom Stuffed Bell Peppers 156

Greek-Style Black-Eyed Peas with Spinach and Tomatoes 157

Moroccan Chickpea and Carrot Tagine 158

Spanish White Bean and Kale Salad with Sherry Vinaigrette 159

Lebanese Mujadara with Lentils and Brown Rice 160

DESSERTS 162

Orange and Almond Flourless Cake 162

Greek Baklava Cheesecake 162

Honey and Pistachio Semolina Cake 164

Date and Walnut Stuffed Figs 165

Lemon Yogurt Parfait with Berries and Mint 165

Pistachio and Olive Oil Cake with Orange Glaze 166

Greek Yogurt and Berry Popsicles 167

Almond Flour and Lemon Zest Biscotti 168

Cardamom and Honey Poached Pears 169

Chocolate Avocado Mousse with Sea Salt 170

Orange Blossom Honey and Almond Tart 171

Greek Yogurt and Lemon Poppy Seed Muffins 172

Pistachio and Fig Energy Bites 173

Olive Oil and Citrus Semolina Cake 174

Dark Chocolate-Dipped Dried Fruits and Nuts 175

Italian Olive Oil and Citrus Cake 176

Mediterranean Chia Seed Pudding with Pomegranate 177

Pistachio and Apricot Protein Balls 178

Moroccan Orange Blossom Water Sorbet 179

Chapter 10 180

Week 1 180

Week 2 181

Week 3 182

Week 4 183

Conclusion 186

Enjoying Your New-Found Mediterranean Lifestyle with Your Air Fryer 186

Recipe Index 187

Introduction

Welcome to the exciting world of the Mediterranean Air Fryer Cookbook! Get ready to explore a delightful fusion of Mediterranean flavors and the easy cooking method of the air fryer. In this introduction, we will explore a Mediterranean adventure where we combine the vibrant flavors, nutritious ingredients, and healthy traditions of the Mediterranean with the simple cooking capabilities of the air fryer.

The Mediterranean Diet and the Air Fryer

The Mediterranean diet is well-known for being healthy and enjoyable, with a good balance of food. The focus is on eating whole grains, fresh fruits and vegetables, lean proteins, and healthy fats like olive oil. This cookbook will show you how the air fryer can help you make delicious and healthy Mediterranean dishes. We will also discuss why the Mediterranean diet promotes a long and healthy life. Additionally, we will discuss how the air fryer can help you make delicious, crispy dishes with less fat.

This introduction marks the start of your journey with the Mediterranean Air Fryer Cookbook. You will find various delicious recipes as you continue reading the following chapters. Each recipe is designed to bring the delicious flavors of the Mediterranean to your table using the air fryer, which makes cooking quick and easy. Prepare to cook some delicious Mediterranean dishes that are tasty and good for you. Put on your apron, preheat your air fryer, and let's get started on this culinary adventure!

Chapter 1

Tips for Air Frying Success

Air frying has become popular for its ability to provide a healthier cooking option compared to traditional deep frying, while still maintaining flavor. To increase the likelihood of success with air frying, here are some essential tips to keep in mind:

Choose the appropriate model: Start by choosing the appropriate air fryer that suits your requirements. Different models have different capacities and features. To make an informed decision, consider the size of your family and the types of food you plan to cook.

Preheat the Air Fryer: Preheating the air fryer is recommended, similar to preheating an oven. It helps to begin cooking your food right away, resulting in a crispy outer layer while keeping the inside moist. Typically, preheat for approximately 5 minutes.

Don't Overcrowd: One common mistake in air frying is overcrowding the basket. To achieve optimal crispiness, it is recommended to leave some space between the food items. Overcrowding can result in uneven cooking and potentially lead to soggier outcomes.

Use a Little Oil: Although air frying is generally considered healthier, it may still require a small amount of oil. To promote browning, lightly coat your food with oil using a cooking spray or a brush. Be careful not to use too much oil, as it can make the result greasy.

Shake or Flip: For even cooking, it is recommended to shake or flip the food halfway through the cooking time. This helps prevent sticking and allows the hot air to evenly reach all sides of your food, resulting in a uniform crisp.

Experiment with Temperature and Time: Air fryers are equipped with adjustable temperature and time settings for conducting experiments with temperature and time. Try experimenting with these ingredients to find the perfect combination for various dishes. Higher temperatures generally produce a crispier texture, while lower temperatures are more appropriate for reheating or dehydrating.

Keep an Eye on Your Food: Pay close attention to your cooking process to ensure the quality of your food. Although air fryers are generally low-maintenance, the cooking times for different foods may vary. Prevent undercooking or burning by closely monitoring the progress of your food.

Use Parchment Paper: To prevent sticking and make cleanup easier, it is recommended to use parchment paper or perforated air fryer liners. This also helps preserve the integrity of delicate or smaller foods.

Get Creative: Air fryers are versatile. Explore a diverse selection of dishes, including traditional favorites like fries and chicken wings, as well as vegetables and baked goods. There are many possibilities.

Clean Regularly: It is important to clean your air fryer thoroughly after every use. Many parts can be safely washed in the dishwasher, making cleanup easy. Regular maintenance helps to maintain the optimal performance of your air fryer.

Following these essential tips can improve your air frying skills, and you can enjoy delicious, healthier meals with a crispy exterior and a tender interior. With practice and experimentation, this kitchen appliance can become your new best friend for quick and wholesome cooking.

Chapter 2

Stocking Your Mediterranean Pantry

The Mediterranean diet is known for its tasty and nutritious cuisine, consisting of fresh ingredients, strong flavors, and a deep cultural heritage. To properly embrace this culinary tradition, having the right ingredients in your pantry is essential. Here's a guide to stocking your pantry with the right Mediterranean ingredients for easy access:

1. Extra Virgin Olive Oil (EVOO): This is commonly used in Mediterranean cooking. Search for high-quality, cold-pressed extra virgin olive oil (EVOO) that can be used in dressings, sautéing, and as a finishing touch for dishes.

2. Herbs and Spices: Mediterranean cuisine commonly includes herbs and spices like oregano, thyme, rosemary, basil, mint, and parsley. Stock both dried and fresh varieties to enhance the flavor of your dishes.

3. Garlic and Onions: Garlic and onions are commonly used in Mediterranean recipes to enhance flavor. Fresh garlic and onions enhance the flavor of soups, stews, and sautéed dishes.

4. Canned Tomatoes: Store whole, diced, and crushed canned tomatoes in your pantry for making quick pasta sauces, soups, and Mediterranean dishes like ratatouille.

5. Pasta and Grains: Stock up on pasta varieties such as penne, spaghetti, and couscous. Additionally, consider including a variety of grains such as bulgur, quinoa, and rice to enhance the flavors of your dishes.

6. Legumes: Legumes such as chickpeas, lentils, and cannellini beans, whether dried or canned, are commonly used in Mediterranean cuisine due to their high protein content.

7. Olives and Capers: Green and black olives, as well as capers, add a savory and tangy flavor to salads, pasta, and sauces.

8. Nuts: Almonds, walnuts, and pine nuts can add a satisfying crunch to salads, pilafs, and desserts.

9. Vinegars: Balsamic vinegar, red wine vinegar, and white wine vinegar are commonly used in dressings, marinades, and to add flavor to dishes.

10. Cheeses: Cheeses commonly used in Mediterranean dishes include Feta, goat cheese, and Parmesan. Creamy and salty flavors are added to your recipes by them.

11. Seafood: Canned tuna and anchovies are commonly used in Mediterranean recipes. They are great for enhancing the umami flavor in dishes.

12. Spreads: Tahini, hummus, and pesto are versatile spreads that can be used for sandwiches, dips, and pasta.

13. Dried Fruits: Dried fruits such as raisins, figs, and apricots are occasionally used in Mediterranean cooking to provide a touch of sweetness to savory dishes.

14. Wine and Spirits: Keep white and red wine for cooking and enjoying with meals. Additionally, consider having some ouzo, a Mediterranean anise-flavored liquor, for a traditional touch.

15. Honey: Natural honey is commonly used in both sweet and savory Mediterranean dishes and desserts.

By stocking your pantry with these Mediterranean essentials, you'll have the necessary ingredients to prepare a variety of delicious dishes that embody the flavors and essence of the Mediterranean region. Experience, appreciate, and delight in the culinary adventure as you discover this cherished cuisine's flavorful and varied tastes.

SALADS

Greek Quinoa Salad with Feta and Kalamata Olives

Prep Time: 15 minutes **Cook Time:** 20 minutes **Number of Servings:** 4

Ingredients:

- 1 cup quinoa, rinsed
- 2 cups water
- 1 cucumber, diced
- 1 cup cherry tomatoes, halved
- 1/2 red onion, finely chopped
- 1/2 cup crumbled feta cheese
- 1/3 cup Kalamata olives, pitted and sliced
- 1/4 cup fresh parsley, chopped
- 2 tablespoons extra-virgin olive oil
- 2 tablespoons fresh lemon juice
- 1 teaspoon dried oregano
- Salt and pepper to taste

Instructions:

1. In a medium saucepan, add the quinoa and water. Bring to a boil, then reduce heat to low, cover, and simmer for about 15-20 minutes, or until the quinoa is cooked and water is absorbed. Take it out from heat and let it cool.
2. In a large mixing bowl, add the cooled quinoa, diced cucumber, halved cherry tomatoes, finely chopped red onion, crumbled feta cheese, and sliced Kalamata olives.
3. In a small bowl, whisk the extra-virgin olive oil, fresh lemon juice, dried oregano, salt, and pepper. Pour this dressing over the salad and gently toss everything together until well combined.
4. Sprinkle the chopped fresh parsley over the salad for added flavor and freshness.
5. Serve immediately, or refrigerate for a few hours to allow the flavors to meld before serving.

Nutritional Information (per serving):

- Carbs: 40g
- Fats: 15g
- Fiber: 6g
- Protein: 10g

Roasted Red Pepper and Chickpea Salad

Prep Time: 10 minutes **Cook Time:** 15 minutes **Number of Servings:** 4

Ingredients:

- 2 large red bell peppers
- 1 can (15 oz) chickpeas, drained and rinsed
- 1/2 red onion, finely diced
- 2 cloves garlic, minced
- 2 tablespoons extra-virgin olive oil
- 1 tablespoon red wine vinegar
- 1 teaspoon dried oregano
- Salt and pepper to taste
- 2 tablespoons fresh parsley, chopped
- 1/4 cup crumbled feta cheese (optional)

Instructions:

1. Preheat your air fryer to 400°F (200°C).
2. Cut the red bell peppers into quarters, removing the seeds and membranes. Place them in the air fryer basket, skin side up, and air fry for about 10-12 minutes or until the pepper skins are charred and blistered. Take them out from the air fryer and let them cool for a few minutes. Once cooled, peel off the skin and slice the roasted peppers into thin strips.
3. In a mixing bowl, add the roasted red pepper strips, drained and rinsed chickpeas, finely diced red onion, and minced garlic.
4. In a separate small bowl, whisk the extra-virgin olive oil, red wine vinegar, dried oregano, salt, and pepper to make the dressing.
5. Pour the dressing over the salad and toss to coat all the ingredients evenly.
6. Sprinkle the chopped fresh parsley over the salad for added flavor and freshness.
7. If desired, top the salad with crumbled feta cheese.
8. Serve immediately or refrigerate until ready to serve.

Nutritional Information (per serving):

- Carbs: 25g
- Fats: 9g
- Fiber: 7g
- Protein: 7g

Watermelon and Mint Salad with Feta

Prep Time: 15 minutes **Cook Time:** 0 minutes **Number of Servings:** 4

Ingredients:

- 4 cups watermelon, diced
- 1/2 cup crumbled feta cheese

- 1/4 cup fresh mint leaves, chopped
- 1 tablespoon extra-virgin olive oil
- 1 tablespoon fresh lime juice
- 1 teaspoon honey
- Salt and pepper to taste

Instructions:

1. In a large mixing bowl, add the diced watermelon, crumbled feta cheese, and chopped fresh mint leaves.
2. In a small bowl, whisk the extra-virgin olive oil, fresh lime juice, honey, salt, and pepper to create the dressing.
3. Pour the dressing over the watermelon, feta, and mint mixture.
4. Gently toss the ingredients together until evenly coated with the dressing.
5. Serve the salad immediately, garnished with extra mint leaves if desired.

Nutritional Information (per serving):

- Carbs: 21g
- Fats: 7g
- Fiber: 1g
- Protein: 4g

Mediterranean Tuna and White Bean Salad

Prep Time: 15 minutes **Cook Time:** 0 minutes **Number of Servings:** 4

Ingredients:

- 2 cans (15 oz each) white beans (cannellini or great northern), drained and rinsed
- 2 cans (5 oz each) tuna in water, drained
- 1 cucumber, diced
- 1 cup cherry tomatoes, halved
- 1/2 red onion, finely chopped
- 1/4 cup Kalamata olives, pitted and sliced
- 2 tablespoons extra-virgin olive oil
- 2 tablespoons fresh lemon juice
- 1 teaspoon dried oregano
- Salt and pepper to taste
- 1/4 cup fresh parsley, chopped
- 1/4 cup crumbled feta cheese (optional)

Instructions:

1. In a large mixing bowl, add the drained and rinsed white beans, flaked tuna, diced cucumber, halved cherry tomatoes, finely chopped

red onion, and sliced Kalamata olives.

2. In a separate small bowl, whisk the extra-virgin olive oil, fresh lemon juice, dried oregano, salt, and pepper to make the dressing.

3. Pour the dressing over the salad ingredients in the large bowl.

4. Gently toss all the ingredients together until well coated with the dressing.

5. Sprinkle the chopped fresh parsley over the salad for added flavor and freshness.

6. If desired, top the salad with crumbled feta cheese.

7. Serve immediately, or refrigerate until ready to serve.

Nutritional Information (per serving):

- Carbs: 38g
- Fats: 12g
- Fiber: 10g
- Protein: 29g

Grilled Halloumi Salad with Fig Vinaigrette

Prep Time: 15 minutes **Cook Time:** 10 minutes **Number of Servings:** 4

Ingredients:

For the Salad:

- 8 slices of halloumi cheese
- 6 cups mixed greens (e.g., arugula, spinach, and baby kale)
- 1 cup cherry tomatoes, halved
- 1/2 red onion, thinly sliced
- 1/4 cup sliced almonds, toasted

For the Fig Vinaigrette:

- 6 dried figs, soaked in hot water for 10 minutes and chopped
- 1/4 cup extra-virgin olive oil
- 2 tablespoons balsamic vinegar
- 1 tablespoon fresh lemon juice
- 1 clove garlic, minced
- Salt and pepper to taste

Instructions:

1. Preheat your air fryer to 400°F (200°C).

2. Place the halloumi cheese slices in the air fryer basket and air fry for 4-5 minutes, flipping halfway through, or until golden brown and slightly crispy. Take it out from the air fryer and set aside.

3. In a large mixing bowl, add the mixed greens, halved cherry tomatoes, thinly

sliced red onion, and toasted sliced almonds.

4. In a blender or food processor, add the chopped dried figs, extra-virgin olive oil, balsamic vinegar, fresh lemon juice, minced garlic, salt, and pepper. Blend until the dressing is smooth and well combined.

5. Drizzle the fig vinaigrette over the salad in the mixing bowl and toss gently to coat all the ingredients with the dressing.

6. Divide the salad among four plates.

7. Top each salad with two slices of grilled halloumi cheese.

8. Serve immediately.

Nutritional Information (per serving):

- Carbs: 20g
- Fats: 28g
- Fiber: 4g
- Protein: 14g

Mediterranean Watercress Salad with Pomegranate and Pistachios

Prep Time: 15 minutes **Cook Time:** 0 minutes **Number of Servings:** 4

Ingredients:

- 4 cups watercress, tough stems removed
- 1 cup pomegranate seeds
- 1/2 cup shelled pistachios
- 1/4 cup red onion, thinly sliced
- 2 tablespoons extra-virgin olive oil
- 1 tablespoon red wine vinegar
- 1 teaspoon honey
- Salt and pepper to taste

Instructions:

1. In a large mixing bowl, add the watercress, pomegranate seeds, shelled pistachios, and thinly sliced red onion.

2. In a separate small bowl, whisk the extra-virgin olive oil, red wine vinegar, honey, salt, and pepper to create the dressing.

3. Pour the dressing over the salad ingredients in the large bowl.

4. Gently toss all the ingredients together until well coated with the dressing.

5. Serve immediately.

Nutritional Information (per serving):

- Carbs: 15g
- Fats: 13g
- Fiber: 3g

- Protein: 5g

Roasted Beet and Quinoa Salad with Citrus Dressing

Prep Time: 15 minutes **Cook Time:** 30 minutes **Number of Servings:** 4

Ingredients:

For the Salad:

- 2 cups quinoa, rinsed
- 4 medium beets, peeled and diced
- 2 tablespoons olive oil
- Salt and pepper to taste
- 1 cup fresh spinach leaves
- 1/2 cup crumbled feta cheese
- 1/4 cup chopped walnuts, toasted
- 2 tablespoons fresh mint leaves, chopped

For the Citrus Dressing:

- Juice of 2 oranges
- Juice of 1 lemon
- 2 tablespoons extra-virgin olive oil
- 1 teaspoon honey
- Salt and pepper to taste

Instructions:

1. Preheat your air fryer to 375°F (190°C).
2. In a large mixing bowl, add the diced beets with olive oil, salt, and pepper. Toss to coat the beets evenly.
3. Place the seasoned beets in the air fryer basket and air fry for 25-30 minutes, shaking the basket occasionally, or until the beets are tender and slightly caramelized. Take it out from the air fryer and let them cool.
4. In a saucepan, add the rinsed quinoa with 4 cups of water. Bring to a boil, then reduce the heat to low, cover, and simmer for 15-20 minutes or until the quinoa is cooked and water is absorbed. Fluff the quinoa with a fork and let it cool.
5. In a large serving bowl, add the cooked quinoa, roasted beets, fresh spinach leaves, crumbled feta cheese, toasted chopped walnuts, and fresh mint leaves.
6. In a separate bowl, whisk the orange juice, lemon juice, extra-virgin olive oil, honey, salt, and pepper to create the citrus dressing.
7. Drizzle the citrus dressing over the salad in the serving bowl.
8. Gently toss all the ingredients together until well coated with the dressing.
9. Serve the salad immediately.

Nutritional Information (per serving):

- Carbs: 54g
- Fats: 19g
- Fiber: 9g
- Protein: 14g

Tabbouleh Salad with Cauliflower Rice

Prep Time: 15 minutes **Cook Time:** 5 minutes **Number of Servings:** 4

Ingredients:

- 1 head of cauliflower, cut into florets
- 1 cup fresh parsley, finely chopped
- 1/2 cup fresh mint leaves, finely chopped
- 1/2 cup cucumber, finely diced
- 1/2 cup cherry tomatoes, finely diced
- 1/4 cup red onion, finely chopped
- 1/4 cup extra-virgin olive oil
- 2 tablespoons fresh lemon juice
- 1 clove garlic, minced
- Salt and pepper to taste

Instructions:

1. Preheat your air fryer to 375°F (190°C).
2. Place the cauliflower florets in the air fryer basket and air fry for 5 minutes or until tender and slightly golden. Take it out from the air fryer and let them cool.
3. In a food processor, pulse the cooled cauliflower florets until they resemble rice-like grains. Transfer the cauliflower rice to a large mixing bowl.
4. To the cauliflower rice, add the finely chopped fresh parsley, finely chopped fresh mint leaves, finely diced cucumber, finely diced cherry tomatoes, and finely chopped red onion.
5. In a small bowl, whisk the extra-virgin olive oil, fresh lemon juice, minced garlic, salt, and pepper to create the dressing.
6. Pour the dressing over the cauliflower rice and vegetable mixture in the large bowl.
7. Gently toss all the ingredients together until well coated with the dressing.
8. Serve the Tabbouleh salad immediately, or refrigerate until ready to serve.

Nutritional Information (per serving):

- Carbs: 9g
- Fats: 11g

- Fiber: 3g
- Protein: 2g

Zucchini Ribbon Salad with Basil Pesto

Prep Time: 15 minutes **Cook Time:** 5 minutes **Number of Servings:** 4

Ingredients:

For the Salad:

- 4 medium zucchini
- 1 cup cherry tomatoes, halved
- 1/4 cup pine nuts, toasted
- 1/4 cup Parmesan cheese, shaved
- Salt and pepper to taste

For the Basil Pesto:

- 2 cups fresh basil leaves
- 1/2 cup extra-virgin olive oil
- 1/4 cup grated Parmesan cheese
- 1/4 cup pine nuts
- 2 cloves garlic, minced
- Salt and pepper to taste
- Juice of 1 lemon

Instructions:

1. Preheat your air fryer to 375°F (190°C).
2. Toast the pine nuts in the air fryer for 2-3 minutes, shaking the basket occasionally, until lightly browned. Take it out from the air fryer and let them cool.
3. Using a vegetable peeler or a mandoline slicer, create thin ribbons from the zucchini. Place the zucchini ribbons in a large mixing bowl.
4. In a food processor, add the fresh basil leaves, extra-virgin olive oil, grated Parmesan cheese, toasted pine nuts, minced garlic, salt, pepper, and the juice of 1 lemon. Blend until you have a smooth basil pesto.
5. Pour the basil pesto over the zucchini ribbons in the large bowl.
6. Toss the zucchini ribbons with the pesto until well coated.
7. Add the halved cherry tomatoes and shaved Parmesan cheese to the salad and gently toss to combine.
8. Season the salad with salt and pepper to taste.
9. Sprinkle the toasted pine nuts over the top for added crunch and flavor.
10. Serve the Zucchini Ribbon Salad with Basil Pesto immediately, or refrigerate until ready to serve.

Nutritional Information (per serving):

- Carbs: 10g
- Fats: 25g
- Fiber: 3g
- Protein: 7g

Radicchio and Blood Orange Salad with Toasted Pine Nuts

Prep Time: 15 minutes **Cook Time:** 3 minutes **Number of Servings:** 4

Ingredients:

For the Salad:

- 1 head of radicchio, thinly sliced
- 3 blood oranges, peeled and sliced
- 1/4 cup pine nuts, toasted
- 1/4 cup red onion, thinly sliced
- Salt and pepper to taste

For the Citrus Dressing:

- Juice of 2 blood oranges
- Juice of 1 lemon
- 2 tablespoons extra-virgin olive oil
- 1 teaspoon honey
- Salt and pepper to taste

Instructions:

1. Preheat your air fryer to 350°F (175°C).
2. Place the pine nuts in the air fryer basket and air fry for 2-3 minutes, shaking the basket occasionally, until lightly toasted. Take it out from the air fryer and let them cool.
3. In a large mixing bowl, add the thinly sliced radicchio, peeled and sliced blood oranges, toasted pine nuts, and thinly sliced red onion.
4. In a separate small bowl, whisk the juice of 2 blood oranges, juice of 1 lemon, extra-virgin olive oil, honey, salt, and pepper to create the citrus dressing.
5. Pour the citrus dressing over the salad in the large bowl.
6. Gently toss all the ingredients together until well coated with the dressing.
7. Season the salad with salt and pepper to taste.
8. Serve the Radicchio and Blood Orange Salad with Toasted Pine Nuts immediately.

Nutritional Information (per serving):

- Carbs: 18g
- Fats: 12g
- Fiber: 4g
- Protein: 3g

Arugula and Roasted Grape Salad with Balsamic Vinaigrette

Prep Time: 10 minutes **Cook Time:** 5 minutes **Number of Servings:** 4

Ingredients:

For the Salad:

- 8 cups arugula
- 2 cups red grapes
- 1/4 cup walnuts, toasted
- 1/4 cup goat cheese, crumbled
- Salt and pepper to taste

For the Balsamic Vinaigrette:

- 1/4 cup balsamic vinegar
- 2 tablespoons extra-virgin olive oil
- 1 teaspoon honey
- 1/2 teaspoon Dijon mustard
- Salt and pepper to taste

Instructions:

1. Preheat your air fryer to 375°F (190°C).
2. Place the red grapes in the air fryer basket and air fry for 4-5 minutes, until slightly caramelized and blistered. Take it out from the air fryer and let them cool.
3. In a large mixing bowl, add the arugula, toasted walnuts, and crumbled goat cheese.
4. To make the balsamic vinaigrette, whisk the balsamic vinegar, extra-virgin olive oil, honey, Dijon mustard, salt, and pepper in a small bowl.
5. Pour the balsamic vinaigrette over the salad in the large bowl.
6. Gently toss all the ingredients together until well coated with the dressing.
7. Add the roasted grapes to the salad and gently mix them in.
8. Season the salad with salt and pepper to taste.
9. Serve the Arugula and Roasted Grape Salad with Balsamic Vinaigrette immediately.

Nutritional Information (per serving):

- Carbs: 18g
- Fats: 13g
- Fiber: 2g
- Protein: 5g

Chickpea and Spinach Salad with Lemon-Tahini Dressing

Prep Time: 15 minutes **Cook Time:** 5 minutes (for toasting chickpeas) **Number of Servings:** 4

Ingredients:

For the Salad:

- 2 cans (15 oz each) chickpeas, drained and rinsed
- 1 tablespoon olive oil
- Salt and pepper to taste
- 8 cups fresh spinach leaves
- 1 cucumber, diced
- 1 red bell pepper, diced
- 1/2 red onion, finely chopped

For the Lemon-Tahini Dressing:

- 1/4 cup tahini
- Juice of 2 lemons
- 2 tablespoons extra-virgin olive oil
- 2 cloves garlic, minced
- Salt and pepper to taste
- Water (to thin dressing, if needed)

Instructions:

1. Preheat your air fryer to 375°F (190°C).
2. In a bowl, toss the drained and rinsed chickpeas with olive oil, salt, and pepper.
3. Place the seasoned chickpeas in the air fryer basket and air fry for 5 minutes until crispy and slightly browned. Take it out from the air fryer and let them cool.
4. In a large mixing bowl, add the fresh spinach leaves, diced cucumber, diced red bell pepper, and finely chopped red onion.
5. To make the Lemon-Tahini Dressing, whisk the tahini, lemon juice, extra-virgin olive oil, minced garlic, salt, and pepper in a small bowl. If the dressing is too thick, you can add a little water to thin it out to your desired consistency.
6. Pour the Lemon-Tahini Dressing over the salad in the large bowl.
7. Gently toss all the salad ingredients together until well coated with the dressing.
8. Add the crispy chickpeas to the salad just before serving to maintain their crunch.
9. Serve the Chickpea and Spinach Salad with Lemon-Tahini Dressing immediately.

Nutritional Information (per serving):

- Carbs: 35g
- Fats: 20g
- Fiber: 10g
- Protein: 14g

Roasted Fennel and Orange Salad with Toasted Hazelnuts

Prep Time: 15 minutes **Cook Time:** 25 minutes **Number of Servings:** 4

Ingredients:

For the Salad:

- 2 large fennel bulbs, thinly sliced
- 3 oranges, peeled and sliced
- 1/2 cup hazelnuts, toasted and roughly chopped
- 4 cups arugula
- Salt and pepper to taste

For the Dressing:

- 3 tablespoons extra-virgin olive oil
- 2 tablespoons fresh lemon juice
- 1 tablespoon honey
- 1 clove garlic, minced
- Salt and pepper to taste

Instructions:

1. Preheat your air fryer to 375°F (190°C).
2. Place the thinly sliced fennel in the air fryer basket and air fry for 20-25 minutes, or until the fennel is tender and slightly caramelized. Take it out from the air fryer and let it cool.
3. While the fennel is cooling, toast the hazelnuts in the air fryer for 2-3 minutes, shaking the basket occasionally, until lightly browned. Take it out from the air fryer and let them cool before roughly chopping.
4. In a large mixing bowl, add the roasted fennel, peeled and sliced oranges, toasted and chopped hazelnuts, and arugula.
5. To make the dressing, whisk the extra-virgin olive oil, fresh lemon juice, honey, minced garlic, salt, and pepper in a small bowl.
6. Pour the dressing over the salad in the large bowl.
7. Gently toss all the salad ingredients together until well coated with the dressing.
8. Season the salad with salt and pepper to taste.
9. Serve the Roasted Fennel and Orange Salad with Toasted Hazelnuts immediately.

Nutritional Information (per serving):

- Carbs: 29g
- Fats: 22g
- Fiber: 8g
- Protein: 5g

Mediterranean Cucumber Ribbon Salad with Dill Yogurt Dressing

Prep Time: 15 minutes **Cook Time:** 0 minutes **Number of Servings:** 4

Ingredients:

For the Salad:

- 3 large cucumbers
- 1/2 cup cherry tomatoes, halved
- 1/4 cup red onion, thinly sliced
- 1/4 cup Kalamata olives, pitted and sliced
- 1/4 cup crumbled feta cheese (optional)
- Salt and pepper to taste

For the Dill Yogurt Dressing:

- 1 cup Greek yogurt
- 2 tablespoons fresh lemon juice
- 1/4 cup fresh dill, finely chopped
- 1 clove garlic, minced
- Salt and pepper to taste

Instructions:

1. Slice off the ends of the cucumbers. Using a vegetable peeler or a mandoline slicer, create thin cucumber ribbons by sliding the peeler or slicer along the length of the cucumbers. Place the cucumber ribbons in a large mixing bowl.
2. Add the halved cherry tomatoes, thinly sliced red onion, and sliced Kalamata olives to the cucumber ribbons in the large bowl.
3. If desired, sprinkle crumbled feta cheese over the salad.
4. In a separate bowl, add the Greek yogurt, fresh lemon juice, finely chopped fresh dill, minced garlic, salt, and pepper to create the Dill Yogurt Dressing.
5. Pour the Dill Yogurt Dressing over the salad ingredients in the large bowl.
6. Gently toss all the ingredients together until well coated with the dressing.
7. Season the salad with salt and pepper to taste.
8. Serve the Mediterranean Cucumber Ribbon Salad with Dill Yogurt Dressing immediately.

Nutritional Information (per serving):

- Carbs: 12g
- Fats: 6g
- Fiber: 2g
- Protein: 8g

Grilled Artichoke and Asparagus Salad with Lemon Herb Vinaigrette

Prep Time: 15 minutes **Cook Time:** 10 minutes **Number of Servings:** 4

Ingredients:

For the Salad:

- 1 bunch asparagus, trimmed
- 2 cans (14 oz each) artichoke hearts, drained and halved

- 2 tablespoons olive oil
- Salt and pepper to taste
- 4 cups mixed greens (e.g., arugula, spinach, and baby kale)
- 1/4 cup red onion, thinly sliced
- 1/4 cup toasted pine nuts

For the Lemon Herb Vinaigrette:

- Juice of 2 lemons
- 1/4 cup extra-virgin olive oil
- 2 tablespoons fresh basil, finely chopped
- 2 tablespoons fresh mint, finely chopped
- 2 cloves garlic, minced
- Salt and pepper to taste

Instructions:

1. Preheat your air fryer to 375°F (190°C).
2. Toss the trimmed asparagus and halved artichoke hearts with olive oil, salt, and pepper in a bowl.
3. Place the seasoned asparagus and artichoke hearts in the air fryer basket and air fry for 8-10 minutes, until tender and slightly charred. Take it out from the air fryer and let them cool.
4. In a large mixing bowl, add the mixed greens, thinly sliced red onion, and toasted pine nuts.
5. To make the Lemon Herb Vinaigrette, whisk the lemon juice, extra-virgin olive oil, finely chopped fresh basil, finely chopped fresh mint, minced garlic, salt, and pepper in a small bowl.
6. Pour the Lemon Herb Vinaigrette over the salad ingredients in the large bowl.
7. Gently toss all the ingredients together until well coated with the dressing.
8. Add the grilled asparagus and artichoke hearts to the salad just before serving.
9. Season the salad with salt and pepper to taste.
10. Serve the Grilled Artichoke and Asparagus Salad with Lemon Herb Vinaigrette immediately.

Nutritional Information (per serving):

- Carbs: 19g
- Fats: 26g
- Fiber: 6g
- Protein: 7g

Roasted Carrot and Chickpea Salad with Cumin-Lemon Dressing

Prep Time: 15 minutes **Cook Time:** 20 minutes **Number of Servings:** 4

Ingredients:

For the Salad:

- 1 pound carrots, peeled and sliced into sticks
- 2 cans (15 oz each) chickpeas, drained and rinsed
- 2 tablespoons olive oil
- Salt and pepper to taste
- 4 cups mixed salad greens (e.g., Romaine, spinach, and arugula)
- 1/4 cup red onion, thinly sliced
- 1/4 cup fresh parsley, chopped
- 1/4 cup almonds, toasted and chopped

For the Cumin-Lemon Dressing:

- Juice of 2 lemons
- 1/4 cup extra-virgin olive oil
- 1 teaspoon ground cumin
- 1 clove garlic, minced
- Salt and pepper to taste

Instructions:

1. Preheat your air fryer to 375°F (190°C).
2. Toss the sliced carrots and chickpeas with olive oil, salt, and pepper in a bowl.
3. Place the seasoned carrots and chickpeas in the air fryer basket and air fry for 18-20 minutes, shaking the basket occasionally, until the carrots are tender and slightly caramelized. Take it out from the air fryer and let them cool.
4. In a large mixing bowl, add the mixed salad greens, thinly sliced red onion, chopped fresh parsley, and toasted chopped almonds.
5. To make the Cumin-Lemon Dressing, whisk the lemon juice, extra-virgin olive oil, ground cumin, minced garlic, salt, and pepper in a small bowl.
6. Pour the Cumin-Lemon Dressing over the salad ingredients in the large bowl.
7. Gently toss all the ingredients together until well coated with the dressing.
8. Add the roasted carrots and chickpeas to the salad just before serving.
9. Season the salad with salt and pepper to taste.
10. Serve the Roasted Carrot and Chickpea Salad with Cumin-Lemon Dressing immediately.

Nutritional Information (per serving):

- Carbs: 35g
- Fats: 26g
- Fiber: 10g
- Protein: 10g

Italian Caprese Salad with Avocado and Balsamic Glaze

Prep Time: 10 minutes **Cook Time:** 5 minutes (for toasting pine nuts)
Number of Servings: 4

Ingredients:

For the Salad:

- 4 large tomatoes, sliced
- 2 ripe avocados, sliced
- 1 cup fresh mozzarella cheese, sliced or cubed
- Fresh basil leaves, for garnish
- Salt and pepper to taste

For the Balsamic Glaze:

- 1/2 cup balsamic vinegar
- 2 tablespoons honey

For the Toasted Pine Nuts (optional):

- 1/4 cup pine nuts

Instructions:

1. Preheat your air fryer to 375°F (190°C).
2. If using pine nuts, place them in the air fryer basket and air fry for 3-5 minutes, shaking the basket occasionally, until lightly browned. Take it out from the air fryer and let them cool.
3. On a large serving platter, arrange the sliced tomatoes, sliced avocados, and fresh mozzarella cheese.
4. If you toasted pine nuts, sprinkle them over the salad.
5. Season the salad with salt and pepper to taste.
6. To make the Balsamic Glaze, add the balsamic vinegar and honey in a small saucepan over low heat. Simmer for 5-7 minutes, or until the mixture has thickened and reduced by half. Take it out from heat and let it cool slightly.
7. Drizzle the Balsamic Glaze over the salad.
8. Garnish with fresh basil leaves.
9. Serve the Italian Caprese Salad with Avocado and Balsamic Glaze immediately.

Nutritional Information (per serving):

- Carbs: 23g
- Fats: 22g
- Fiber: 8g
- Protein: 14g

Greek Tuna and White Bean Salad with Dill

Prep Time: 15 minutes **Cook Time:** 0 minutes (no cooking required)
Number of Servings: 4

Ingredients:

For the Salad:

- 2 cans (15 oz each) white beans (cannellini or Great Northern), drained and rinsed
- 2 cans (5 oz each) tuna in water, drained
- 1 cup cherry tomatoes, halved
- 1/2 cup cucumber, diced
- 1/4 cup red onion, finely chopped
- 1/4 cup Kalamata olives, pitted and sliced
- 1/4 cup fresh dill, finely chopped
- Salt and pepper to taste

For the Lemon Dijon Dressing:

- Juice of 2 lemons
- 2 tablespoons extra-virgin olive oil
- 1 tablespoon Dijon mustard
- 1 clove garlic, minced
- Salt and pepper to taste

Instructions:

1. In a large mixing bowl, add the drained and rinsed white beans, drained tuna, halved cherry tomatoes, diced cucumber, finely chopped red onion, sliced Kalamata olives, and finely chopped fresh dill.
2. To make the Lemon Dijon Dressing, whisk the lemon juice, extra-virgin olive oil, Dijon mustard, minced garlic, salt, and pepper in a small bowl.
3. Pour the Lemon Dijon Dressing over the salad in the large bowl.
4. Gently toss all the salad ingredients together until well coated with the dressing.
5. Season the salad with salt and pepper to taste.
6. Serve the Greek Tuna and White Bean Salad with Dill immediately.

Nutritional Information (per serving):

- Carbs: 45g
- Fats: 11g
- Fiber: 11g
- Protein: 32g

Moroccan Spiced Cauliflower Salad with Tahini

Prep Time: 15 minutes **Cook Time:** 15 minutes **Number of Servings:** 4

Ingredients:

For the Salad:

- 1 large cauliflower head, cut into florets
- 2 tablespoons olive oil
- 1 teaspoon ground cumin

- 1 teaspoon ground coriander
- 1/2 teaspoon ground paprika
- 1/2 teaspoon ground cinnamon
- Salt and pepper to taste
- 1/4 cup fresh cilantro leaves, chopped
- 1/4 cup fresh mint leaves, chopped
- 1/4 cup pomegranate seeds
- 1/4 cup toasted almonds, chopped

For the Tahini Dressing:

- 1/4 cup tahini
- Juice of 2 lemons
- 2 cloves garlic, minced
- 2 tablespoons extra-virgin olive oil
- Salt and pepper to taste
- Water (to thin dressing, if needed)

Instructions:

1. Preheat your air fryer to 375°F (190°C).
2. In a large bowl, toss the cauliflower florets with olive oil, ground cumin, ground coriander, ground paprika, ground cinnamon, salt, and pepper.
3. Place the seasoned cauliflower florets in the air fryer basket and air fry for 12-15 minutes, shaking the basket occasionally, until tender and slightly caramelized. Take it out from the air fryer and let them cool.
4. In a large mixing bowl, add the roasted cauliflower, chopped fresh cilantro, chopped fresh mint, pomegranate seeds, and chopped toasted almonds.
5. To make the Tahini Dressing, whisk the tahini, lemon juice, minced garlic, extra-virgin olive oil, salt, and pepper in a small bowl. If the dressing is too thick, you can add a little water to thin it out to your desired consistency.
6. Pour the Tahini Dressing over the salad in the large bowl.
7. Gently toss all the salad ingredients together until well coated with the dressing.
8. Season the salad with salt and pepper to taste.
9. Serve the Moroccan Spiced Cauliflower Salad with Tahini immediately.

Nutritional Information (per serving):

- Carbs: 21g
- Fats: 24g
- Fiber: 8g

- Protein: 9g

Mediterranean Watermelon Radish and Mint Salad

Prep Time: 15 minutes **Cook Time:** 0 minutes (no cooking required)
Number of Servings: 4

Ingredients:

- 1 small watermelon, seeded and cubed
- 3-4 medium watermelon radishes, thinly sliced
- 1/4 cup fresh mint leaves, chopped
- 1/4 cup red onion, thinly sliced
- 1/4 cup feta cheese, crumbled (optional)
- Salt and pepper to taste
- Juice of 1 lime

Instructions:

1. In a large mixing bowl, add the cubed watermelon, thinly sliced watermelon radishes, chopped fresh mint leaves, and thinly sliced red onion.
2. If desired, sprinkle crumbled feta cheese over the salad.
3. Season the salad with salt and pepper to taste.
4. Squeeze the juice of 1 lime over the salad.
5. Gently toss all the salad ingredients together until well combined.
6. Serve the Mediterranean Watermelon Radish and Mint Salad immediately.

Nutritional Information (per serving):

- Carbs: 29g
- Fats: 1g
- Fiber: 3g
- Protein: 2g

SOUPS

Spicy Moroccan Lentil Soup

Prep Time: 15 minutes

Cook Time: 30 minutes

Servings: 4

Ingredients:

- 1 cup dried red lentils
- 1 onion, diced
- 2 cloves garlic, minced
- 1 carrot, diced
- 1 celery stalk, diced
- 1 red bell pepper, diced
- 1 teaspoon ground cumin
- 1 teaspoon ground coriander
- 1/2 teaspoon ground turmeric
- 1/2 teaspoon smoked paprika
- 1/4 teaspoon cayenne pepper (adjust to taste)
- 1 can (14 ounces) diced tomatoes
- 4 cups low-sodium vegetable broth
- 1 tablespoon olive oil
- Salt and pepper to taste
- Fresh cilantro leaves for garnish (optional)

Instructions:

1. Rinse the dried red lentils thoroughly in a fine-mesh sieve and set them aside.

2. Heat the olive oil in an air fryer set to 360°F (180°C). Add the diced onion, minced garlic, diced carrot, diced celery, and diced red bell pepper to the air fryer basket. Cook for 5 minutes, shaking the basket occasionally to ensure even cooking.

3. Stir in the ground cumin, ground coriander, ground turmeric, smoked paprika, and cayenne pepper into the air fryer basket with the sautéed vegetables. Cook for an extra 2 minutes to toast the spices, stirring occasionally.

4. Add the rinsed red lentils, diced tomatoes, and low-sodium vegetable broth to the air fryer basket. Stir sufficiently to combine all the ingredients.

5. Close the air fryer basket and cook the soup at 360°F (180°C) for 20-25 minutes, or until the lentils and vegetables are tender. Stir the soup occasionally during cooking.

6. Once the soup is done, season it with salt and pepper to taste.

7. Serve the Spicy Moroccan Lentil Soup hot, garnished with fresh cilantro leaves if desired.

Nutritional Information (per serving):

- Carbs: 30g
- Fats: 3g
- Fiber: 9g
- Protein: 11g

Lemon Chicken Orzo Soup with Spinach

Prep Time: 15 minutes

Cook Time: 25 minutes

Servings: 4

Ingredients:

- 1 cup uncooked whole wheat orzo pasta
- 2 boneless, skinless chicken breasts, diced
- 1 onion, diced
- 2 cloves garlic, minced
- 1 carrot, sliced
- 1 celery stalk, sliced
- 4 cups low-sodium chicken broth
- 1 lemon, zest and juice
- 2 cups fresh spinach leaves
- 1 teaspoon dried thyme
- 1 bay leaf
- Salt and pepper to taste
- 1 tablespoon olive oil
- Fresh parsley leaves for garnish (optional)

Instructions:

1. Preheat your air fryer to 400°F (200°C).

2. Season the diced chicken breasts with salt and pepper.

3. Place the seasoned chicken in the air fryer basket and cook for 10-12 minutes, shaking the basket halfway through, until the chicken is properly cooked and nicely browned. Take out the chicken from the air fryer and set it aside.

4. In a large pot on the stove, heat the olive oil over medium heat. Add the diced onion, minced garlic, sliced carrot, and sliced celery. Sauté for about 5 minutes until the vegetables soften.

5. Add the chicken broth, lemon zest, lemon juice, dried thyme, and bay leaf to the pot. Bring the mixture to a simmer.

6. Stir in the uncooked whole wheat orzo pasta and simmer for 8-10 minutes, or until the orzo is tender but still slightly al dente.

7. Add the cooked chicken back into the pot and simmer for an extra 2-3 minutes until the chicken is heated through.

8. Stir in the fresh spinach leaves and cook for 1-2 minutes until wilted.

9. Take out the bay leaf and season the soup with additional salt and pepper to taste.

10. Serve the Lemon Chicken Orzo Soup with Spinach hot, garnished with fresh parsley leaves if desired.

Nutritional Information (per serving):

- Carbs: 38g
- Fats: 6g
- Fiber: 6g
- Protein: 27g

Greek Avgolemono Soup with Shrimp

Prep Time: 15 minutes

Cook Time: 20 minutes

Servings: 4

Ingredients:

- 1 pound large shrimp, peeled and deveined
- 1 cup uncooked orzo pasta
- 1 onion, diced
- 2 cloves garlic, minced
- 4 cups low-sodium chicken broth
- 1/2 cup fresh lemon juice (from about 2-3 lemons)
- 2 large eggs
- 1/4 cup fresh dill, chopped
- Salt and pepper to taste
- Olive oil for sautéing
- Lemon wedges for garnish (optional)

Instructions:

1. Preheat your air fryer to 400°F (200°C).

2. Season the shrimp with a pinch of salt and pepper.

3. Place the seasoned shrimp in the air fryer basket and cook for 4-6 minutes, until the shrimp are pink and properly cooked. Take out the shrimp from the air fryer and set them aside.

4. In a large pot on the stove, heat a bit of olive oil over medium heat. Add the diced onion and minced garlic. Sauté for about 3 minutes until the onions become translucent.

5. Add the uncooked orzo pasta to the pot and continue to sauté for another 2-3 minutes until the orzo is lightly toasted.

6. Pour in the low-sodium chicken broth and bring the mixture to a boil. Reduce the heat and simmer for 10-12 minutes, or until the orzo is tender.

7. In a separate bowl, whisk the fresh lemon juice and eggs until well combined.

8. Gradually add a ladleful of the hot soup broth into the lemon and egg mixture, whisking constantly to temper the eggs.

9. Slowly pour the tempered egg mixture back into the pot, stirring continuously. This will thicken the soup without curdling the eggs.

10. Stir in the cooked shrimp and chopped fresh dill. Cook for an extra 2-3 minutes until the shrimp are heated through.

11. Season the Greek Avgolemono Soup with Shrimp with additional salt and pepper to taste.

12. Serve the soup hot, garnished with lemon wedges if desired.

Nutritional Information (per serving):

- Carbs: 41g
- Fats: 7g
- Fiber: 2g
- Protein: 27g

Roasted Tomato and Basil Soup with White Beans

Prep Time: 15 minutes

Cook Time: 25 minutes

Servings: 4

Ingredients:

- 4 cups fresh tomatoes, halved
- 1 onion, sliced
- 3 cloves garlic, minced
- 2 tablespoons olive oil
- 1 can (15 ounces) white beans, drained and rinsed
- 2 cups low-sodium vegetable broth
- 1/4 cup fresh basil leaves, chopped
- 1 teaspoon dried oregano
- Salt and pepper to taste
- Balsamic vinegar for drizzling (optional)
- Fresh basil leaves for garnish (optional)

Instructions:

1. Preheat your air fryer to 375°F (190°C).

2. In a large bowl, add the halved fresh tomatoes, sliced onion, minced garlic, and olive oil. Toss to coat the vegetables evenly with the oil.

3. Place the tomato mixture in the air fryer basket and roast for 15-18 minutes, shaking the basket occasionally, until the tomatoes are soft and slightly caramelized.

4. Take out the roasted tomato mixture from the air fryer and transfer it to a blender or food processor. Blend until smooth.

5. In a large pot on the stove, add the blended tomato mixture, drained white beans, low-sodium vegetable broth, dried oregano, and chopped fresh basil leaves.

6. Bring the mixture to a simmer over medium heat and let it cook for 5-7 minutes, allowing the flavors to meld.

7. Season the soup with salt and pepper to taste.

8. Serve the Roasted Tomato and Basil Soup with White Beans hot, drizzled with balsamic vinegar and garnished with fresh basil leaves if desired.

Nutritional Information (per serving):

- Carbs: 26g
- Fats: 6g
- Fiber: 7g
- Protein: 6g

Tuscan Ribollita Soup with Kale

Prep Time: 20 minutes

Cook Time: 30 minutes

Servings: 4

Ingredients:

- 1 can (15 ounces) cannellini beans, drained and rinsed
- 1 cup diced tomatoes (canned or fresh)
- 1 onion, diced
- 2 cloves garlic, minced
- 1 carrot, diced
- 1 celery stalk, diced
- 4 cups low-sodium vegetable broth
- 2 cups kale, chopped
- 1 cup whole-grain bread, cubed
- 2 tablespoons olive oil
- 1 teaspoon dried rosemary
- 1 teaspoon dried thyme
- Salt and pepper to taste
- Grated Parmesan cheese for garnish (optional)

Instructions:

1. Preheat your air fryer to 375°F (190°C).

2. In a large bowl, toss the cubed whole-grain bread with one tablespoon of olive oil, dried rosemary, and

dried thyme until the bread is coated.

3. Place the seasoned bread cubes in the air fryer basket and roast for 5-7 minutes, shaking the basket occasionally, until the bread is crisp and golden. Take out the croutons from the air fryer and set them aside.
4. In a large pot on the stove, heat the remaining one tablespoon of olive oil over medium heat. Add the diced onion, minced garlic, diced carrot, and diced celery. Sauté for about 5 minutes until the vegetables soften.
5. Add the diced tomatoes and cook for an extra 2-3 minutes.
6. Stir in the cannellini beans and low-sodium vegetable broth. Bring the mixture to a simmer.
7. Add the chopped kale to the pot and let it cook for 5-7 minutes until wilted and tender.
8. Season the soup with salt and pepper to taste.
9. Serve the Tuscan Ribollita Soup with Kale hot, garnished with the air-fried croutons and grated Parmesan cheese if desired.

Nutritional Information (per serving):

- Carbs: 31g
- Fats: 7g
- Fiber: 7g
- Protein: 8g

Spanish Gazpacho with Avocado Salsa

Prep Time: 20 minutes

Cook Time: 0 minutes (No cooking required)

Servings: 4

Ingredients:

For Gazpacho:

- 4 large ripe tomatoes, diced
- 1 cucumber, peeled, seeded, and diced
- 1 red bell pepper, diced
- 1/2 red onion, diced
- 2 cloves garlic, minced
- 3 cups low-sodium tomato juice
- 2 tablespoons red wine vinegar
- 2 tablespoons extra-virgin olive oil
- 1 teaspoon dried oregano
- Salt and pepper to taste

For Avocado Salsa:

- 2 ripe avocados, diced
- 1/4 cup red onion, finely chopped

- 1/4 cup fresh cilantro leaves, chopped
- Juice of 1 lime
- Salt and pepper to taste

Instructions:

For Gazpacho:

1. In a large bowl, add the diced tomatoes, diced cucumber, diced red bell pepper, diced red onion, and minced garlic.
2. In a blender or food processor, add half of the vegetable mixture along with the low-sodium tomato juice, red wine vinegar, extra-virgin olive oil, dried oregano, salt, and pepper. Blend until smooth.
3. Pour the blended mixture back into the bowl with the remaining diced vegetables. Stir to combine.
4. Refrigerate the Gazpacho for at least 2 hours or until well chilled. Chilling allows the flavors to meld.

For Avocado Salsa:

1. In a separate bowl, add the diced avocados, finely chopped red onion, chopped cilantro leaves, lime juice, salt, and pepper.
2. Gently toss the ingredients to combine, being careful not to mash the avocados too much.

To Serve:

1. Ladle the chilled Gazpacho into bowls.
2. Top each serving with a generous spoonful of the Avocado Salsa.
3. Garnish with additional cilantro leaves if desired.

Nutritional Information (per serving):

- Carbs: 23g
- Fats: 15g
- Fiber: 8g
- Protein: 4g

Mediterranean Lentil and Spinach Soup

Prep Time: 15 minutes

Cook Time: 30 minutes

Servings: 4

Ingredients:

- 1 cup dried green or brown lentils
- 1 onion, diced
- 2 cloves garlic, minced
- 1 carrot, diced
- 1 celery stalk, diced
- 1 red bell pepper, diced
- 4 cups low-sodium vegetable broth

- 1 can (14 ounces) diced tomatoes
- 2 cups fresh spinach leaves
- 1 teaspoon dried oregano
- 1/2 teaspoon dried thyme
- 1/2 teaspoon smoked paprika
- Salt and pepper to taste
- 1 tablespoon olive oil
- Lemon wedges for garnish (optional)

Instructions:

1. Rinse the dried lentils thoroughly in a fine-mesh sieve and set them aside.
2. Heat the olive oil in your air fryer to 360°F (180°C).
3. Add the diced onion, minced garlic, diced carrot, diced celery, and diced red bell pepper to the air fryer basket. Cook for 5 minutes, shaking the basket occasionally to ensure even cooking.
4. Stir in the dried oregano, dried thyme, and smoked paprika into the air fryer basket with the sautéed vegetables. Cook for an extra 2 minutes to toast the spices, stirring occasionally.
5. Add the rinsed lentils, diced tomatoes, and low-sodium vegetable broth to the air fryer basket. Stir sufficiently to combine all the ingredients.
6. Close the air fryer basket and cook the soup at 360°F (180°C) for 20-25 minutes, or until the lentils are tender. Stir the soup occasionally during cooking.
7. Once the lentils are cooked, season the soup with salt and pepper to taste.
8. Stir in the fresh spinach leaves and cook for an extra 1-2 minutes until wilted.
9. Serve the Mediterranean Lentil and Spinach Soup hot, garnished with lemon wedges if desired.

Nutritional Information (per serving):

- Carbs: 36g
- Fats: 4g
- Fiber: 11g
- Protein: 12g

Roasted Eggplant and Tomato Soup

Prep Time: 15 minutes

Cook Time: 30 minutes

Servings: 4

Ingredients:

- 1 large eggplant, diced
- 4 ripe tomatoes, diced
- 1 onion, diced

- 2 cloves garlic, minced
- 2 tablespoons olive oil
- 4 cups low-sodium vegetable broth
- 1 teaspoon dried basil
- 1 teaspoon dried oregano
- Salt and pepper to taste
- Fresh basil leaves for garnish (optional)

Instructions:

1. Preheat your air fryer to 375°F (190°C).
2. In a large bowl, toss the diced eggplant and diced tomatoes with one tablespoon of olive oil, dried basil, dried oregano, salt, and pepper until the vegetables are well coated.
3. Place the seasoned eggplant and tomato mixture in the air fryer basket and roast for 15-18 minutes, shaking the basket occasionally, until the vegetables are tender and slightly caramelized. Take out the roasted vegetables from the air fryer and set them aside.
4. In a large pot on the stove, heat the remaining one tablespoon of olive oil over medium heat. Add the diced onion and minced garlic. Sauté for about 5 minutes until the onions become translucent.
5. Add the roasted eggplant and tomato mixture to the pot.
6. Pour in the low-sodium vegetable broth and bring the mixture to a simmer.
7. Simmer the soup for 10-12 minutes to allow the flavors to meld.
8. Season the Roasted Eggplant and Tomato Soup with salt and pepper to taste.
9. Serve the soup hot, garnished with fresh basil leaves if desired.

Nutritional Information (per serving):

- Carbs: 20g
- Fats: 6g
- Fiber: 7g
- Protein: 3g

Greek Lemon Chickpea Soup

Prep Time: 15 minutes

Cook Time: 30 minutes

Servings: 4

Ingredients:

- 1 cup dried chickpeas, soaked and drained
- 1 onion, finely chopped
- 2 cloves garlic, minced
- 2 carrots, diced
- 2 celery stalks, diced

- 1 lemon, zest and juice
- 4 cups low-sodium vegetable broth
- 1 teaspoon dried oregano
- 1/2 teaspoon ground cumin
- Salt and pepper to taste
- 2 tablespoons olive oil
- Fresh parsley leaves for garnish (optional)

Instructions:

1. Preheat your air fryer to 375°F (190°C).
2. In a large bowl, toss the soaked and drained chickpeas with one tablespoon of olive oil, dried oregano, ground cumin, salt, and pepper until well coated.
3. Place the seasoned chickpeas in the air fryer basket and roast for 15-20 minutes, shaking the basket occasionally, until the chickpeas are crispy and golden. Take out the roasted chickpeas from the air fryer and set them aside.
4. In a large pot on the stove, heat the remaining one tablespoon of olive oil over medium heat. Add the finely chopped onion, minced garlic, diced carrots, and diced celery. Sauté for about 5 minutes until the vegetables soften.
5. Add the lemon zest to the pot and sauté for an extra minute to release the aroma.
6. Pour in the low-sodium vegetable broth and bring the mixture to a boil.
7. Reduce the heat to a simmer and add the soaked and drained chickpeas to the pot. Simmer for 15-20 minutes, or until the chickpeas are tender.
8. Stir in the lemon juice and season the Greek Lemon Chickpea Soup with salt and pepper to taste.
9. Serve the soup hot, garnished with roasted chickpeas and fresh parsley leaves if desired.

Nutritional Information (per serving):

- Carbs: 29g
- Fats: 7g
- Fiber: 7g
- Protein: 8g

Italian White Bean and Kale Soup with Turkey Sausage

Prep Time: 15 minutes

Cook Time: 30 minutes

Servings: 4

Ingredients:

- 1 cup dried white beans (cannellini or Great

Northern), soaked and drained

- 2 turkey sausage links, sliced into rounds
- 1 onion, diced
- 2 cloves garlic, minced
- 2 carrots, diced
- 2 celery stalks, diced
- 4 cups low-sodium chicken broth
- 2 cups kale, chopped
- 1 teaspoon dried basil
- 1/2 teaspoon dried thyme
- Salt and pepper to taste
- 1 tablespoon olive oil
- Grated Parmesan cheese for garnish (optional)

Instructions:

1. Preheat your air fryer to 375°F (190°C).
2. In a large bowl, toss the soaked and drained white beans with one tablespoon of olive oil, dried basil, dried thyme, salt, and pepper until well coated.
3. Place the seasoned white beans in the air fryer basket and roast for 15-20 minutes, shaking the basket occasionally, until the beans are crispy and lightly golden. Take out the roasted beans from the air fryer and set them aside.
4. In a large pot on the stove, cook the sliced turkey sausage rounds over medium heat until browned and properly cooked. Take out the sausage from the pot and set it aside.
5. In the same pot, add the diced onion, minced garlic, diced carrots, and diced celery. Sauté for about 5 minutes until the vegetables soften.
6. Pour in the low-sodium chicken broth and bring the mixture to a boil.
7. Reduce the heat to a simmer and add the soaked and drained white beans to the pot. Simmer for 15-20 minutes, or until the beans are tender.
8. Stir in the chopped kale and cooked turkey sausage. Cook for an extra 5 minutes until the kale is wilted.
9. Season the Italian White Bean and Kale Soup with Turkey Sausage with salt and pepper to taste.
10. Serve the soup hot, garnished with roasted white beans and grated Parmesan cheese if desired.

Nutritional Information (per serving):

- Carbs: 29g
- Fats: 6g

- Fiber: 8g
- Protein: 15g

Tomato and Basil Quinoa Soup

Prep Time: 15 minutes

Cook Time: 25 minutes

Servings: 4

Ingredients:

- 1 cup quinoa, rinsed and drained
- 4 cups low-sodium vegetable broth
- 1 onion, diced
- 2 cloves garlic, minced
- 4 tomatoes, diced
- 1/2 cup fresh basil leaves, chopped
- 1 teaspoon dried oregano
- Salt and pepper to taste
- 1 tablespoon olive oil
- Grated Parmesan cheese for garnish (optional)

Instructions:

1. Preheat your air fryer to 375°F (190°C).
2. In a large bowl, toss the rinsed and drained quinoa with one tablespoon of olive oil, dried oregano, salt, and pepper until well coated.
3. Place the seasoned quinoa in the air fryer basket and roast for 12-15 minutes, shaking the basket occasionally, until the quinoa is toasted and golden. Take out the roasted quinoa from the air fryer and set it aside.
4. In a large pot on the stove, heat a bit of olive oil over medium heat. Add the diced onion and minced garlic. Sauté for about 5 minutes until the onions become translucent.
5. Add the diced tomatoes to the pot and cook for an extra 2-3 minutes.
6. Pour in the low-sodium vegetable broth and bring the mixture to a boil.
7. Reduce the heat to a simmer and add the roasted quinoa to the pot. Simmer for 12-15 minutes, or until the quinoa is cooked and tender.
8. Stir in the chopped fresh basil leaves.
9. Season the Tomato and Basil Quinoa Soup with salt and pepper to taste.
10. Serve the soup hot, garnished with grated Parmesan cheese if desired.

Nutritional Information (per serving):

- Carbs: 42g
- Fats: 6g

- Fiber: 6g
- Protein: 8g

Lebanese Red Lentil and Spinach Soup

Prep Time: 15 minutes

Cook Time: 25 minutes

Servings: 4

Ingredients:

- 1 cup dried red lentils, rinsed and drained
- 4 cups low-sodium vegetable broth
- 1 onion, finely chopped
- 2 cloves garlic, minced
- 2 carrots, diced
- 2 celery stalks, diced
- 4 cups fresh spinach leaves
- 1 teaspoon ground cumin
- 1/2 teaspoon ground coriander
- Salt and pepper to taste
- 2 tablespoons olive oil
- Lemon wedges for garnish (optional)

Instructions:

1. Preheat your air fryer to 375°F (190°C).
2. In a large bowl, toss the rinsed and drained red lentils with one tablespoon of olive oil, ground cumin, ground coriander, salt, and pepper until well coated.
3. Place the seasoned red lentils in the air fryer basket and roast for 12-15 minutes, shaking the basket occasionally, until the lentils are crispy and golden. Take out the roasted lentils from the air fryer and set them aside.
4. In a large pot on the stove, heat the remaining one tablespoon of olive oil over medium heat. Add the finely chopped onion and minced garlic. Sauté for about 5 minutes until the onions become translucent.
5. Add the diced carrots and diced celery to the pot. Sauté for an extra 5 minutes until the vegetables soften.
6. Pour in the low-sodium vegetable broth and bring the mixture to a boil.
7. Reduce the heat to a simmer and add the roasted red lentils to the pot. Simmer for 12-15 minutes, or until the lentils are tender.
8. Stir in the fresh spinach leaves and cook for an extra 1-2 minutes until wilted.
9. Season the Lebanese Red Lentil and Spinach Soup with salt and pepper to taste.

10. Serve the soup hot, garnished with lemon wedges if desired.

Nutritional Information (per serving):

- Carbs: 36g
- Fats: 6g
- Fiber: 10g
- Protein: 12g

Greek Lemon Rice Soup with Kale

Prep Time: 15 minutes

Cook Time: 25 minutes

Servings: 4

Ingredients:

- 1/2 cup long-grain white rice
- 4 cups low-sodium chicken broth
- 1 onion, finely chopped
- 2 cloves garlic, minced
- 2 cups kale, chopped
- 2 eggs
- Juice of 2 lemons
- 1 teaspoon dried dill
- Salt and pepper to taste
- Olive oil for drizzling (optional)

Instructions:

1. Preheat your air fryer to 375°F (190°C).
2. In a large bowl, toss the long-grain white rice with one tablespoon of olive oil. Place the rice in the air fryer basket and roast for 5-7 minutes, shaking the basket occasionally, until the rice is lightly toasted. Take out the roasted rice from the air fryer and set it aside.
3. In a large pot on the stove, heat a bit of olive oil over medium heat. Add the finely chopped onion and minced garlic. Sauté for about 5 minutes until the onions become translucent.
4. Pour in the low-sodium chicken broth and bring it to a boil.
5. Stir in the toasted rice and dried dill. Reduce the heat to a simmer and cook for 15-18 minutes, or until the rice is tender.
6. In a small bowl, beat the eggs until well combined.
7. Slowly add the lemon juice to the beaten eggs, whisking continuously to temper the eggs.
8. Gradually pour the tempered egg mixture back into the pot, stirring continuously. This will thicken the soup without curdling the eggs.
9. Stir in the chopped kale and cook for an extra 2-3

minutes until the kale is wilted.

10. Season the Greek Lemon Rice Soup with Kale with salt and pepper to taste.

11. Serve the soup hot, drizzled with a bit of olive oil if desired.

Nutritional Information (per serving):

- Carbs: 31g
- Fats: 5g
- Fiber: 2g
- Protein: 7g

Spanish White Bean and Garlic Soup

Prep Time: 15 minutes

Cook Time: 30 minutes

Servings: 4

Ingredients:

- 2 cups dried white beans (Great Northern or cannellini), soaked and drained
- 1 onion, finely chopped
- 6 cloves garlic, minced
- 2 bay leaves
- 4 cups low-sodium vegetable broth
- 1 teaspoon smoked paprika
- 1/2 teaspoon dried thyme
- Salt and pepper to taste
- 2 tablespoons olive oil
- Fresh parsley leaves for garnish (optional)

Instructions:

1. Preheat your air fryer to 375°F (190°C).

2. In a large bowl, toss the soaked and drained white beans with one tablespoon of olive oil. Place the beans in the air fryer basket and roast for 15-18 minutes, shaking the basket occasionally, until the beans are crispy and golden. Take out the roasted beans from the air fryer and set them aside.

3. In a large pot on the stove, heat the remaining one tablespoon of olive oil over medium heat. Add the finely chopped onion and minced garlic. Sauté for about 5 minutes until the onions become translucent.

4. Add the bay leaves, smoked paprika, and dried thyme to the pot. Sauté for an extra 2 minutes to release the flavors.

5. Pour in the low-sodium vegetable broth and bring it to a boil.

6. Stir in the roasted white beans and reduce the heat to a simmer. Let the soup cook for 15-20 minutes, allowing the flavors to meld.

7. Season the Spanish White Bean and Garlic Soup with salt and pepper to taste.

8. Serve the soup hot, garnished with fresh parsley leaves if desired.

Nutritional Information (per serving):

- Carbs: 31g
- Fats: 6g
- Fiber: 7g
- Protein: 9g

Moroccan Chickpea and Spinach Stew

Prep Time: 15 minutes

Cook Time: 30 minutes

Servings: 4

Ingredients:

- 2 cups dried chickpeas, soaked and drained
- 1 onion, finely chopped
- 2 cloves garlic, minced
- 2 carrots, diced
- 2 celery stalks, diced
- 1 red bell pepper, diced
- 4 cups low-sodium vegetable broth
- 1 can (14 ounces) diced tomatoes
- 2 cups fresh spinach leaves
- 1 teaspoon ground cumin
- 1/2 teaspoon ground coriander
- 1/2 teaspoon ground cinnamon
- Salt and pepper to taste
- 2 tablespoons olive oil
- Lemon wedges for garnish (optional)

Instructions:

1. Preheat your air fryer to 375°F (190°C).

2. In a large bowl, toss the soaked and drained chickpeas with one tablespoon of olive oil, ground cumin, ground coriander, ground cinnamon, salt, and pepper until well coated.

3. Place the seasoned chickpeas in the air fryer basket and roast for 15-20 minutes, shaking the basket occasionally, until the chickpeas are crispy and golden. Take out the roasted chickpeas from the air fryer and set them aside.

4. In a large pot on the stove, heat the remaining one tablespoon of olive oil over medium heat. Add the finely chopped onion and minced garlic. Sauté for about 5 minutes until the onions become translucent.

5. Add the diced carrots, diced celery, and diced red bell pepper to the pot. Sauté for an extra 5 minutes until the vegetables soften.
6. Pour in the low-sodium vegetable broth and bring the mixture to a boil.
7. Stir in the diced tomatoes and the roasted chickpeas. Reduce the heat to a simmer and cook for 15-20 minutes, allowing the flavors to meld.
8. Stir in the fresh spinach leaves and cook for an extra 2-3 minutes until the spinach is wilted.
9. Season the Moroccan Chickpea and Spinach Stew with salt and pepper to taste.
10. Serve the stew hot, garnished with lemon wedges if desired.

Nutritional Information (per serving):

- Carbs: 38g
- Fats: 7g
- Fiber: 11g
- Protein: 11g

Italian Minestrone Soup with Cannellini Beans

Prep Time: 15 minutes

Cook Time: 30 minutes

Servings: 4

Ingredients:

- 1 cup dried cannellini beans, soaked and drained
- 1 onion, finely chopped
- 2 cloves garlic, minced
- 2 carrots, diced
- 2 celery stalks, diced
- 1 zucchini, diced
- 4 cups low-sodium vegetable broth
- 1 can (14 ounces) diced tomatoes
- 1 cup green beans, cut into 1-inch pieces
- 1 cup small pasta (such as ditalini or macaroni)
- 1 teaspoon dried basil
- 1/2 teaspoon dried oregano
- Salt and pepper to taste
- 2 tablespoons olive oil
- Grated Parmesan cheese for garnish (optional)

Instructions:

1. Preheat your air fryer to 375°F (190°C).
2. In a large bowl, toss the soaked and drained cannellini beans with one tablespoon of olive oil, dried basil, dried oregano, salt, and pepper until well coated.
3. Place the seasoned cannellini beans in the air fryer basket

and roast for 15-18 minutes, shaking the basket occasionally, until the beans are crispy and golden. Take out the roasted beans from the air fryer and set them aside.

4. In a large pot on the stove, heat the remaining one tablespoon of olive oil over medium heat. Add the finely chopped onion and minced garlic. Sauté for about 5 minutes until the onions become translucent.

5. Add the diced carrots, diced celery, and diced zucchini to the pot. Sauté for an extra 5 minutes until the vegetables soften.

6. Pour in the low-sodium vegetable broth and bring the mixture to a boil.

7. Stir in the diced tomatoes, green beans, and small pasta. Simmer for 10-12 minutes, or until the pasta is cooked and the vegetables are tender.

8. Stir in the roasted cannellini beans and cook for an extra 2-3 minutes to heat through.

9. Season the Italian Minestrone Soup with Cannellini Beans with salt and pepper to taste.

10. Serve the soup hot, garnished with grated Parmesan cheese if desired.

Nutritional Information (per serving):

- Carbs: 54g
- Fats: 7g
- Fiber: 13g
- Protein: 12g

Mediterranean Lentil and Swiss Chard Soup

Prep Time: 15 minutes

Cook Time: 30 minutes

Servings: 4

Ingredients:

- 1 cup dried green or brown lentils, rinsed and drained
- 4 cups low-sodium vegetable broth
- 1 onion, finely chopped
- 2 cloves garlic, minced
- 2 carrots, diced
- 2 celery stalks, diced
- 4 cups Swiss chard leaves, chopped (stems removed)
- 1 can (14 ounces) diced tomatoes
- 1 teaspoon dried thyme
- 1/2 teaspoon dried rosemary
- Salt and pepper to taste
- 2 tablespoons olive oil
- Lemon wedges for garnish (optional)

Instructions:

1. Preheat your air fryer to 375°F (190°C).

2. In a large bowl, toss the rinsed and drained lentils with one tablespoon of olive oil, dried thyme, dried rosemary, salt, and pepper until well coated.

3. Place the seasoned lentils in the air fryer basket and roast for 12-15 minutes, shaking the basket occasionally, until the lentils are toasted and lightly browned. Take out the roasted lentils from the air fryer and set them aside.

4. In a large pot on the stove, heat the remaining one tablespoon of olive oil over medium heat. Add the finely chopped onion and minced garlic. Sauté for about 5 minutes until the onions become translucent.

5. Add the diced carrots and diced celery to the pot. Sauté for an extra 5 minutes until the vegetables soften.

6. Pour in the low-sodium vegetable broth and bring the mixture to a boil.

7. Stir in the diced tomatoes and chopped Swiss chard leaves (stems removed). Simmer for 10-12 minutes, or until the lentils and vegetables are tender.

8. Stir in the roasted lentils and cook for an extra 2-3 minutes to heat through.

9. Season the Mediterranean Lentil and Swiss Chard Soup with salt and pepper to taste.

10. Serve the soup hot, garnished with lemon wedges if desired.

Nutritional Information (per serving):

- Carbs: 38g
- Fats: 7g
- Fiber: 14g
- Protein: 14g

Spanish Chilled Almond and Garlic Soup (Ajo Blanco)

Prep Time: 15 minutes

Cook Time: 0 minutes (no cooking required)

Servings: 4

Ingredients:

- 1 cup blanched almonds
- 2 slices of stale white bread, crusts removed
- 4 cloves garlic, minced
- 2 cups cold water
- 1/4 cup white wine vinegar
- 1/4 cup extra-virgin olive oil
- Salt to taste

- Grapes or sliced almonds for garnish (optional)

Instructions:

1. In a food processor or blender, add the blanched almonds, stale white bread, and minced garlic.

2. Blend the mixture until it forms a smooth paste.

3. While the blender or food processor is running, gradually add the cold water and white wine vinegar. Continue to blend until the mixture is well combined and has a creamy consistency.

4. With the blender or food processor still running, slowly drizzle in the extra-virgin olive oil. Blend until the soup is fully emulsified and creamy.

5. Taste the soup and add salt to your liking. Blend briefly to incorporate the salt.

6. Transfer the Spanish Chilled Almond and Garlic Soup (Ajo Blanco) to a bowl or container, cover, and refrigerate for at least 2 hours to chill.

7. Before serving, give the soup a good stir, as it may thicken while chilling. If it's too thick, you can add a bit of cold water to reach your desired consistency.

8. Serve the chilled soup in bowls, garnished with grapes or sliced almonds if desired.

Nutritional Information (per serving):

- Carbs: 15g
- Fats: 35g
- Fiber: 4g
- Protein: 9g

Greek Lemon Orzo Soup with Spinach and Chicken

Prep Time: 15 minutes

Cook Time: 20 minutes

Servings: 4

Ingredients:

- 1 cup orzo pasta
- 4 cups low-sodium chicken broth
- 1 pound boneless, skinless chicken breasts, diced
- 1 onion, finely chopped
- 2 cloves garlic, minced
- 4 cups fresh spinach leaves
- Juice of 2 lemons
- 1/2 teaspoon dried dill
- Salt and pepper to taste
- Olive oil for drizzling (optional)

Instructions:

1. Preheat your air fryer to 375°F (190°C).

2. In a large bowl, toss the orzo pasta with one tablespoon of olive oil. Place the orzo pasta in the air fryer basket and roast for 5-7 minutes, shaking the basket occasionally, until the pasta is lightly toasted. Take out the roasted orzo pasta from the air fryer and set it aside.

3. In a large pot on the stove, heat a bit of olive oil over medium heat. Add the finely chopped onion and minced garlic. Sauté for about 5 minutes until the onions become translucent.

4. Add the diced chicken to the pot and cook for 5-7 minutes until it's no longer pink and properly cooked.

5. Pour in the low-sodium chicken broth and bring it to a boil.

6. Stir in the roasted orzo pasta and dried dill. Reduce the heat to a simmer and cook for 10-12 minutes, or until the orzo pasta is cooked to your liking.

7. Stir in the fresh spinach leaves and cook for an extra 2-3 minutes until the spinach is wilted.

8. Season the Greek Lemon Orzo Soup with Spinach and Chicken with salt and pepper to taste.

9. Stir in the lemon juice to brighten the flavors.

10. Serve the soup hot, drizzled with a bit of olive oil if desired.

Nutritional Information (per serving):

- Carbs: 32g
- Fats: 5g
- Fiber: 3g
- Protein: 28g

Moroccan Harira Soup with Quinoa

Prep Time: 15 minutes

Cook Time: 30 minutes

Servings: 4

Ingredients:

- 1/2 cup quinoa
- 1 onion, finely chopped
- 2 cloves garlic, minced
- 2 carrots, diced
- 2 celery stalks, diced
- 1 red bell pepper, diced
- 4 cups low-sodium vegetable broth
- 1 can (14 ounces) diced tomatoes
- 1 can (14 ounces) chickpeas, drained and rinsed
- 1/2 cup red lentils

- 1 teaspoon ground cumin
- 1/2 teaspoon ground coriander
- 1/2 teaspoon ground cinnamon
- Salt and pepper to taste
- 2 tablespoons olive oil
- Fresh cilantro leaves for garnish (optional)

Instructions:

1. Preheat your air fryer to 375°F (190°C).
2. Rinse the quinoa thoroughly in a fine-mesh strainer under cold water. Drain well.
3. In a large bowl, toss the rinsed and drained quinoa with one tablespoon of olive oil. Place the quinoa in the air fryer basket and roast for 5-7 minutes, shaking the basket occasionally, until the quinoa is lightly toasted. Take out the roasted quinoa from the air fryer and set it aside.
4. In a large pot on the stove, heat the remaining one tablespoon of olive oil over medium heat. Add the finely chopped onion and minced garlic. Sauté for about 5 minutes until the onions become translucent.
5. Add the diced carrots, diced celery, and diced red bell pepper to the pot. Sauté for an extra 5 minutes until the vegetables soften.
6. Pour in the low-sodium vegetable broth and bring the mixture to a boil.
7. Stir in the diced tomatoes, chickpeas, red lentils, ground cumin, ground coriander, and ground cinnamon. Simmer for 15-20 minutes, or until the lentils and vegetables are tender.
8. Stir in the roasted quinoa and cook for an extra 2-3 minutes to heat through.
9. Season the Moroccan Harira Soup with Quinoa with salt and pepper to taste.
10. Serve the soup hot, garnished with fresh cilantro leaves if desired.

Nutritional Information (per serving):

- Carbs: 45g
- Fats: 8g
- Fiber: 12g
- Protein: 12g

SEAFOOD

Harissa Spiced Grilled Swordfish

Prep Time: 15 minutes

Cook Time: 10 minutes

Servings: 4

Ingredients:

- 4 swordfish fillets (6 ounces each)
- 2 tablespoons harissa paste
- 2 tablespoons olive oil
- 1 teaspoon ground cumin
- 1 teaspoon ground coriander
- 1/2 teaspoon ground paprika
- 1/2 teaspoon ground cayenne pepper
- 2 cloves garlic, minced
- Juice of 1 lemon
- Salt and pepper to taste
- Lemon wedges and fresh cilantro for garnish

Instructions:

1. In a bowl, add the harissa paste, olive oil, ground cumin, ground coriander, ground paprika, ground cayenne pepper, minced garlic, and the juice of 1 lemon. Mix sufficiently to create a marinade.
2. Place the swordfish fillets in a shallow dish and season them with salt and pepper.
3. Pour the harissa marinade over the swordfish fillets, ensuring evenly coated. Cover the dish and refrigerate for at least 30 minutes to marinate.
4. Preheat your air fryer to 400°F (200°C).
5. Take out the swordfish fillets from the marinade and place them in the air fryer basket. You may want to lightly spray the basket with cooking spray to prevent sticking.
6. Air fry the swordfish for about 8-10 minutes, depending on the thickness of the fillets, flipping them halfway through the cooking time. The swordfish should be opaque and flake easily with a fork when done.
7. While the swordfish is cooking, you can brush some of the remaining marinade on top for extra flavor.
8. Once cooked, take out the swordfish from the air fryer.
9. Garnish with lemon wedges and fresh cilantro before serving.

Nutritional Information (per serving):

- Carbs: 2 grams
- Fats: 12 grams
- Fiber: 1 gram
- Protein: 36 grams

Moroccan Baked Fish with Preserved Lemon and Olives

Prep Time: 15 minutes

Cook Time: 15 minutes

Servings: 4

Ingredients:

- 4 white fish fillets (such as cod or tilapia), about 6 ounces each
- 1 preserved lemon, pulp removed and rind thinly sliced
- 1/2 cup green olives, pitted and sliced
- 2 cloves garlic, minced
- 1 teaspoon ground cumin
- 1 teaspoon ground coriander
- 1/2 teaspoon ground paprika
- 1/2 teaspoon ground cinnamon
- 1/4 teaspoon ground cayenne pepper (adjust to taste)
- 2 tablespoons olive oil
- Salt and pepper to taste
- Fresh cilantro leaves for garnish

Instructions:

1. Preheat your air fryer to 375°F (190°C).
2. In a bowl, add the minced garlic, ground cumin, ground coriander, ground paprika, ground cinnamon, ground cayenne pepper, olive oil, and a pinch of salt and pepper. Mix sufficiently to create a marinade.
3. Pat the fish fillets dry with paper towels and place them in a shallow dish.
4. Pour the marinade over the fish fillets, ensuring evenly coated. Allow them to marinate for about 10 minutes.
5. While the fish is marinating, prepare the preserved lemon by removing the pulp and thinly slicing the rind. Also, slice the green olives.
6. After marinating, place the marinated fish fillets in the air fryer basket, leaving some space between them.
7. Add the preserved lemon slices and sliced green olives on top of the fish fillets.
8. Air fry for approximately 12-15 minutes, depending on the thickness of the fillets, until the fish flakes easily with a fork and has a golden brown crust.

9. Garnish with fresh cilantro leaves before serving.

Nutritional Information (per serving):

- Carbs: 4 grams
- Fats: 13 grams
- Fiber: 2 grams
- Protein: 32 grams

Garlic and Herb Shrimp Skewers

Prep Time: 20 minutes

Cook Time: 8 minutes

Servings: 4

Ingredients:

- 1 pound large shrimp, peeled and deveined
- 2 cloves garlic, minced
- 2 tablespoons fresh parsley, chopped
- 1 tablespoon fresh oregano, chopped
- 2 tablespoons olive oil
- 1 lemon, zest and juice
- Salt and pepper to taste
- Wooden skewers, soaked in water for 30 minutes

Instructions:

1. In a bowl, add the minced garlic, chopped fresh parsley, chopped fresh oregano, olive oil, and the zest and juice of 1 lemon. Mix sufficiently to create a marinade.
2. Add the peeled and deveined shrimp to the marinade, ensuring evenly coated. Let them marinate for about 10 minutes.
3. Preheat your air fryer to 400°F (200°C).
4. While the shrimp is marinating, thread them onto the soaked wooden skewers, leaving space between each shrimp.
5. Season the shrimp skewers with a pinch of salt and pepper.
6. Place the shrimp skewers in the air fryer basket, ensuring not overcrowded.
7. Air fry for approximately 6-8 minutes, turning the skewers halfway through the cooking time, until the shrimp are pink and opaque.
8. Serve the garlic and herb shrimp skewers hot, garnished with additional fresh parsley and lemon wedges if desired.

Nutritional Information (per serving):

- Carbs: 3 grams
- Fats: 7 grams
- Fiber: 1 gram
- Protein: 23 grams

Greek-style Stuffed Calamari

Prep Time: 30 minutes

Cook Time: 15 minutes

Servings: 4

Ingredients:

- 8 small calamari tubes, cleaned and tentacles reserved
- 1 cup cooked quinoa
- 1/2 cup diced tomatoes
- 1/4 cup diced red onion
- 1/4 cup diced cucumber
- 1/4 cup chopped fresh parsley
- 1/4 cup chopped fresh dill
- 2 cloves garlic, minced
- 2 tablespoons olive oil
- 1 lemon, zest and juice
- Salt and pepper to taste
- Wooden toothpicks

Instructions:

1. In a bowl, add the cooked quinoa, diced tomatoes, diced red onion, diced cucumber, chopped fresh parsley, chopped fresh dill, minced garlic, olive oil, and the zest and juice of 1 lemon. Mix sufficiently to create the stuffing mixture.
2. Carefully stuff each calamari tube with the prepared stuffing mixture. Be sure not to overfill them.
3. Close the open end of each stuffed calamari tube with a wooden toothpick to secure the stuffing.
4. Preheat your air fryer to 375°F (190°C).
5. Place the stuffed calamari tubes and reserved tentacles in the air fryer basket, ensuring not overcrowded.
6. Air fry for approximately 12-15 minutes, turning them halfway through the cooking time, until the calamari is tender and the stuffing is heated through.
7. Take out the toothpicks before serving.
8. Garnish with additional fresh dill and lemon wedges if desired.

Nutritional Information (per serving):

- Carbs: 19 grams
- Fats: 7 grams
- Fiber: 3 grams
- Protein: 17 grams

Baked Cod with Mediterranean Tomato Sauce

Prep Time: 15 minutes

Cook Time: 20 minutes

Servings: 4

Ingredients:

- 4 cod fillets (6 ounces each)
- 1 can (14 ounces) diced tomatoes, drained
- 1/2 cup diced red onion
- 1/2 cup diced bell pepper (any color)
- 2 cloves garlic, minced
- 1 teaspoon dried oregano
- 1/2 teaspoon dried basil
- 1/2 teaspoon dried thyme
- 1/4 teaspoon crushed red pepper flakes (adjust to taste)
- 2 tablespoons olive oil
- Salt and pepper to taste
- Fresh basil leaves for garnish

Instructions:

1. Preheat your air fryer to 375°F (190°C).
2. In a bowl, add the drained diced tomatoes, diced red onion, diced bell pepper, minced garlic, dried oregano, dried basil, dried thyme, crushed red pepper flakes, olive oil, and a pinch of salt and pepper. Mix sufficiently to create the Mediterranean tomato sauce.
3. Pat the cod fillets dry with paper towels and place them in a shallow dish.
4. Pour the Mediterranean tomato sauce over the cod fillets, ensuring evenly coated. Let them marinate for about 10 minutes.
5. After marinating, place the cod fillets in the air fryer basket, leaving some space between them.
6. Air fry for approximately 18-20 minutes, depending on the thickness of the fillets, until the cod is flaky and has a golden brown crust.
7. Garnish with fresh basil leaves before serving.

Nutritional Information (per serving):

- Carbs: 10 grams
- Fats: 9 grams
- Fiber: 3 grams
- Protein: 30 grams

Baked Lemon Herb Haddock

Prep Time: 10 minutes

Cook Time: 12 minutes

Servings: 4

Ingredients:

- 4 haddock fillets (6 ounces each)
- 2 tablespoons olive oil
- Juice of 1 lemon
- 2 cloves garlic, minced

- 2 tablespoons fresh parsley, chopped
- 1 teaspoon dried dill
- 1/2 teaspoon dried thyme
- 1/2 teaspoon dried rosemary
- Salt and pepper to taste
- Lemon slices for garnish

Instructions:

1. Preheat your air fryer to 375°F (190°C).
2. In a bowl, add the olive oil, lemon juice, minced garlic, chopped fresh parsley, dried dill, dried thyme, dried rosemary, and a pinch of salt and pepper. Mix sufficiently to create the herb and lemon marinade.
3. Place the haddock fillets in a shallow dish.
4. Pour the herb and lemon marinade over the haddock fillets, ensuring evenly coated. Let them marinate for about 5-10 minutes.
5. After marinating, place the haddock fillets in the air fryer basket, leaving some space between them.
6. Air fry for approximately 10-12 minutes, depending on the thickness of the fillets, until the haddock is opaque and flakes easily with a fork.
7. Garnish with lemon slices before serving.

Nutritional Information (per serving):

- Carbs: 2 grams
- Fats: 7 grams
- Fiber: 0 grams
- Protein: 31 grams

Moroccan Chermoula Grilled Prawns

Prep Time: 20 minutes

Cook Time: 8 minutes

Servings: 4

Ingredients:

- 1 pound large prawns, peeled and deveined
- 1/4 cup fresh cilantro, chopped
- 1/4 cup fresh parsley, chopped
- 2 cloves garlic, minced
- 1 teaspoon ground cumin
- 1 teaspoon ground coriander
- 1/2 teaspoon ground paprika
- 1/2 teaspoon ground cayenne pepper
- 1/4 teaspoon ground cinnamon
- Juice of 1 lemon
- 2 tablespoons olive oil
- Salt and pepper to taste
- Lemon wedges for garnish

Instructions:

1. In a bowl, add the chopped fresh cilantro, chopped fresh parsley, minced garlic, ground cumin, ground coriander, ground paprika, ground cayenne pepper, ground cinnamon, juice of 1 lemon, olive oil, and a pinch of salt and pepper. This mixture will become the chermoula marinade.

2. Pat the peeled and deveined prawns dry with paper towels.

3. Place the prawns in the chermoula marinade, ensuring evenly coated. Let them marinate for about 10 minutes.

4. Preheat your air fryer to 400°F (200°C).

5. Thread the marinated prawns onto skewers, leaving a small space between each prawn.

6. Place the prawn skewers in the air fryer basket, ensuring not overcrowded.

7. Air fry for approximately 6-8 minutes, turning the skewers halfway through the cooking time, until the prawns are pink and opaque.

8. Serve the Moroccan Chermoula Grilled Prawns hot, garnished with lemon wedges.

Nutritional Information (per serving):

- Carbs: 2 grams
- Fats: 6 grams
- Fiber: 1 gram
- Protein: 21 grams

Greek Stuffed Sole with Spinach and Feta

Prep Time: 25 minutes

Cook Time: 10 minutes

Servings: 4

Ingredients:

- 4 sole fillets (6 ounces each)
- 2 cups fresh spinach, chopped
- 1/2 cup crumbled feta cheese
- 2 cloves garlic, minced
- 1/4 cup diced red onion
- 1/4 cup diced tomatoes
- 1/4 cup chopped fresh parsley
- 2 tablespoons olive oil
- Juice of 1 lemon
- 1/2 teaspoon dried oregano
- Salt and pepper to taste
- Lemon wedges for garnish

Instructions:

1. Preheat your air fryer to 375°F (190°C).

2. In a skillet over medium heat, add one tablespoon of olive oil. Sauté the minced garlic and diced red onion until softened, about 2 minutes.

3. Add the chopped fresh spinach to the skillet and cook until wilted, about 3 minutes. Take it out from heat.

4. In a bowl, add the sautéed spinach, crumbled feta cheese, diced tomatoes, chopped fresh parsley, juice of 1 lemon, dried oregano, and a pinch of salt and pepper. This mixture will be the stuffing.

5. Lay the sole fillets flat and divide the stuffing mixture equally among them, placing the stuffing in the center of each fillet.

6. Fold the sides of the sole fillets over the stuffing, securing them with toothpicks if necessary.

7. Brush the stuffed sole fillets with the remaining one tablespoon of olive oil.

8. Place the stuffed sole fillets in the air fryer basket, ensuring not overcrowded.

9. Air fry for approximately 8-10 minutes, depending on the thickness of the fillets, until the sole is opaque and flakes easily with a fork.

10. Serve the Greek Stuffed Sole with Spinach and Feta hot, garnished with lemon wedges.

Nutritional Information (per serving):

- Carbs: 5 grams
- Fats: 12 grams
- Fiber: 2 grams
- Protein: 34 grams

Sardine and Olive Tapenade Stuffed Bell Peppers

Prep Time: 20 minutes

Cook Time: 15 minutes

Servings: 4

Ingredients:

- 4 large bell peppers (any color)
- 2 cans (3.75 ounces each) sardines in olive oil, drained and mashed
- 1/2 cup black olives, pitted and finely chopped
- 1/4 cup diced red onion
- 2 cloves garlic, minced
- 1/4 cup chopped fresh parsley
- 2 tablespoons olive oil
- Juice of 1 lemon

- Salt and pepper to taste
- Fresh basil leaves for garnish

Instructions:

1. Preheat your air fryer to 375°F (190°C).
2. Cut the tops off the bell peppers and take out the seeds and membranes from the inside.
3. In a bowl, add the mashed sardines, finely chopped black olives, diced red onion, minced garlic, chopped fresh parsley, olive oil, juice of 1 lemon, and a pinch of salt and pepper. This mixture will be the sardine and olive tapenade.
4. Stuff each bell pepper with the sardine and olive tapenade mixture, pressing it down gently to ensure it's well-packed.
5. Place the stuffed bell peppers in the air fryer basket.
6. Air fry for approximately 12-15 minutes, until the bell peppers are tender and slightly charred.
7. Garnish the Sardine and Olive Tapenade Stuffed Bell Peppers with fresh basil leaves before serving.

Nutritional Information (per serving):

- Carbs: 14 grams
- Fats: 17 grams
- Fiber: 5 grams
- Protein: 14 grams

Tuscan-style Clam and Cannellini Bean Stew

Prep Time: 15 minutes

Cook Time: 15 minutes

Servings: 4

Ingredients:

- 2 cans (14 ounces each) canned clams, drained and juice reserved
- 2 cans (15 ounces each) cannellini beans, drained and rinsed
- 1/2 cup diced onion
- 1/2 cup diced celery
- 1/2 cup diced carrots
- 2 cloves garlic, minced
- 2 tablespoons olive oil
- 1 can (14 ounces) diced tomatoes
- 1 teaspoon dried thyme
- 1 teaspoon dried rosemary
- Salt and pepper to taste
- Fresh parsley for garnish

Instructions:

1. Preheat your air fryer to 375°F (190°C).
2. In a skillet over medium heat, add one tablespoon of

olive oil. Sauté the diced onion, diced celery, and diced carrots until they start to soften, about 5 minutes.

3. Add the minced garlic and sauté for another 1-2 minutes until fragrant. Take it out from heat.

4. In a bowl, add the drained canned clams, drained and rinsed cannellini beans, diced tomatoes, dried thyme, dried rosemary, and the sautéed vegetables. Mix sufficiently to create the stew base.

5. Pour the reserved clam juice into the mixture and stir to combine. This will add flavor to the stew.

6. Drizzle the remaining one tablespoon of olive oil into the air fryer basket.

7. Transfer the stew mixture into the air fryer basket and spread it evenly.

8. Air fry for approximately 12-15 minutes, stirring occasionally, until the stew is heated through and the flavors meld together.

9. Season with salt and pepper to taste.

10. Garnish the Tuscan-style Clam and Cannellini Bean Stew with fresh parsley before serving.

Nutritional Information (per serving):

- Carbs: 33 grams
- Fats: 8 grams
- Fiber: 8 grams
- Protein: 15 grams

Lemon Dill Baked Salmon with Asparagus

Prep Time: 10 minutes

Cook Time: 12 minutes

Servings: 4

Ingredients:

- 4 salmon fillets (6 ounces each)
- 1 bunch asparagus spears, trimmed
- 2 tablespoons olive oil
- Juice of 1 lemon
- Zest of 1 lemon
- 2 cloves garlic, minced
- 2 tablespoons fresh dill, chopped
- Salt and pepper to taste
- Lemon slices for garnish

Instructions:

1. Preheat your air fryer to 375°F (190°C).

2. In a bowl, add the olive oil, lemon juice, lemon zest, minced garlic, chopped fresh dill, and a pinch of salt and pepper. This mixture will be the marinade.

3. Place the salmon fillets in a shallow dish.

4. Pour half of the marinade over the salmon fillets, ensuring evenly coated. Reserve the other half of the marinade for the asparagus.

5. In a separate bowl, toss the trimmed asparagus spears with the reserved marinade.

6. Lay the salmon fillets and marinated asparagus in the air fryer basket, ensuring not overcrowded.

7. Air fry for approximately 10-12 minutes, depending on the thickness of the salmon fillets, until the salmon is opaque and flakes easily with a fork, and the asparagus is tender-crisp.

8. Garnish the Lemon Dill Baked Salmon with Asparagus with lemon slices before serving.

Nutritional Information (per serving):

- Carbs: 6 grams
- Fats: 18 grams
- Fiber: 2 grams
- Protein: 32 grams

Spanish Grilled Mackerel with Romesco Sauce

Prep Time: 20 minutes

Cook Time: 10 minutes

Servings: 4

Ingredients:

For the Mackerel:

- 4 mackerel fillets (6 ounces each)
- 2 tablespoons olive oil
- Juice of 1 lemon
- 2 cloves garlic, minced
- 1 teaspoon smoked paprika
- Salt and pepper to taste

For the Romesco Sauce:

- 1/2 cup roasted red bell peppers, peeled and chopped
- 1/4 cup almonds, toasted
- 2 cloves garlic, minced
- 2 tablespoons olive oil
- 1 tablespoon red wine vinegar
- 1 teaspoon smoked paprika
- Salt and pepper to taste

Instructions:

1. Preheat your air fryer to 375°F (190°C).

2. In a bowl, add the olive oil, lemon juice, minced garlic, smoked paprika, salt, and pepper. This mixture will be the marinade for the mackerel.

3. Place the mackerel fillets in a shallow dish.

4. Pour the marinade over the mackerel fillets, ensuring evenly coated. Let them marinate for about 10 minutes.

5. In the meantime, prepare the Romesco sauce. In a food processor, add the roasted red bell peppers, toasted almonds, minced garlic, olive oil, red wine vinegar, smoked paprika, salt, and pepper. Blend until smooth. Adjust the seasoning to taste.

6. Lay the marinated mackerel fillets in the air fryer basket.

7. Air fry for approximately 8-10 minutes, depending on the thickness of the fillets, until the mackerel is opaque and flakes easily with a fork.

8. Serve the Spanish Grilled Mackerel with a generous drizzle of Romesco sauce.

Nutritional Information (per serving):

- Carbs: 7 grams
- Fats: 26 grams
- Fiber: 3 grams
- Protein: 34 grams

Italian Stuffed Calamari with Spinach and Pine Nuts

Prep Time: 30 minutes

Cook Time: 15 minutes

Servings: 4

Ingredients:

For the Stuffed Calamari:

- 8 large calamari tubes
- 2 cups fresh spinach, chopped
- 1/4 cup pine nuts, toasted
- 1/4 cup diced onion
- 2 cloves garlic, minced
- 2 tablespoons olive oil
- 1/4 cup grated Parmesan cheese
- Salt and pepper to taste

For the Tomato Sauce:

- 1 can (14 ounces) diced tomatoes
- 2 cloves garlic, minced
- 1 teaspoon dried basil
- 1 teaspoon dried oregano
- Salt and pepper to taste

Instructions:

1. Preheat your air fryer to 375°F (190°C).

2. Start by preparing the stuffed calamari. In a skillet over medium heat, add one tablespoon of olive oil. Sauté the diced onion and minced garlic until they become translucent, about 2 minutes.

3. Add the chopped fresh spinach to the skillet and cook until wilted, about 3

minutes. Take it out from heat.

4. In a bowl, add the sautéed spinach, toasted pine nuts, grated Parmesan cheese, and a pinch of salt and pepper. This mixture will be the stuffing for the calamari.

5. Carefully stuff each calamari tube with the prepared spinach and pine nut mixture. Be sure not to overfill them.

6. Close the open end of each stuffed calamari tube with a toothpick to secure the stuffing.

7. Place the stuffed calamari tubes in the air fryer basket.

8. In a separate bowl, add the diced tomatoes, minced garlic, dried basil, dried oregano, salt, and pepper. This will be the tomato sauce.

9. Pour the tomato sauce over the stuffed calamari in the air fryer basket.

10. Air fry for approximately 12-15 minutes, turning the calamari halfway through the cooking time, until the calamari is tender and the sauce is heated through.

11. Take out the toothpicks before serving.

Nutritional Information (per serving):

- Carbs: 15 grams
- Fats: 11 grams
- Fiber: 4 grams
- Protein: 22 grams

Greek Baked Red Snapper with Mediterranean Salsa

Prep Time: 20 minutes

Cook Time: 15 minutes

Servings: 4

Ingredients:

For the Red Snapper:

- 4 red snapper fillets (6 ounces each)
- 2 tablespoons olive oil
- Juice of 1 lemon
- 2 cloves garlic, minced
- 1 teaspoon dried oregano
- Salt and pepper to taste

For the Mediterranean Salsa:

- 1 cup diced tomatoes
- 1/2 cup diced cucumber
- 1/4 cup diced red onion
- 1/4 cup chopped Kalamata olives
- 1/4 cup crumbled feta cheese
- 2 tablespoons chopped fresh parsley
- 2 tablespoons olive oil

- Juice of 1 lemon
- Salt and pepper to taste

Instructions:

1. Preheat your air fryer to 375°F (190°C).
2. In a bowl, add the olive oil, lemon juice, minced garlic, dried oregano, salt, and pepper. This mixture will be the marinade for the red snapper.
3. Place the red snapper fillets in a shallow dish.
4. Pour the marinade over the red snapper fillets, ensuring evenly coated. Let them marinate for about 10 minutes.
5. In the meantime, prepare the Mediterranean salsa. In a separate bowl, add the diced tomatoes, diced cucumber, diced red onion, chopped Kalamata olives, crumbled feta cheese, chopped fresh parsley, olive oil, lemon juice, salt, and pepper. Mix sufficiently to create the salsa.
6. Lay the marinated red snapper fillets in the air fryer basket.
7. Air fry for approximately 10-12 minutes, depending on the thickness of the fillets, until the red snapper is opaque and flakes easily with a fork.
8. Serve the Greek Baked Red Snapper with a generous spoonful of Mediterranean salsa.

Nutritional Information (per serving):

- Carbs: 8 grams
- Fats: 19 grams
- Fiber: 2 grams
- Protein: 35 grams

Harissa Shrimp and Zucchini Noodles

Prep Time: 15 minutes

Cook Time: 10 minutes

Servings: 4

Ingredients:

For the Harissa Shrimp:

- 1 pound large shrimp, peeled and deveined
- 2 tablespoons harissa paste
- 2 cloves garlic, minced
- 1 tablespoon olive oil
- Juice of 1 lemon
- Salt and pepper to taste

For the Zucchini Noodles:

- 4 medium zucchinis, spiralized into noodles
- 2 tablespoons olive oil
- 2 cloves garlic, minced
- 1/2 teaspoon dried oregano

- Salt and pepper to taste

Instructions:

1. Preheat your air fryer to 375°F (190°C).

2. In a bowl, add the harissa paste, minced garlic, olive oil, lemon juice, salt, and pepper. This mixture will be the marinade for the shrimp.

3. Add the peeled and deveined shrimp to the marinade, ensuring evenly coated. Let them marinate for about 10 minutes.

4. In a separate bowl, toss the spiralized zucchini noodles with olive oil, minced garlic, dried oregano, salt, and pepper. This will be the base for your dish.

5. Lay the marinated shrimp in the air fryer basket, leaving some space between them.

6. Air fry for approximately 5-6 minutes, until the shrimp are pink and opaque.

7. In the meantime, place the prepared zucchini noodles in the air fryer basket as well, alongside the shrimp.

8. Air fry for an extra 4-5 minutes, tossing the noodles once during cooking, until the noodles are tender-crisp.

9. Serve the Harissa Shrimp over the Zucchini Noodles.

Nutritional Information (per serving):

- Carbs: 12 grams
- Fats: 10 grams
- Fiber: 3 grams
- Protein: 25 grams

Grilled Swordfish with Italian Salsa Verde

Prep Time: 15 minutes

Cook Time: 10 minutes

Servings: 4

Ingredients:

For the Grilled Swordfish:

- 4 swordfish steaks (6 ounces each)
- 2 tablespoons olive oil
- Juice of 1 lemon
- 2 cloves garlic, minced
- 1 teaspoon dried oregano
- Salt and pepper to taste

For the Italian Salsa Verde:

- 1/2 cup fresh parsley, finely chopped
- 2 tablespoons capers, chopped
- 2 cloves garlic, minced
- 2 tablespoons olive oil
- Juice of 1 lemon
- Salt and pepper to taste

Instructions:

1. Preheat your air fryer to 375°F (190°C).

2. In a bowl, add the olive oil, lemon juice, minced garlic, dried oregano, salt, and pepper. This mixture will be the marinade for the swordfish.

3. Place the swordfish steaks in a shallow dish.

4. Pour the marinade over the swordfish steaks, ensuring evenly coated. Let them marinate for about 10 minutes.

5. In the meantime, prepare the Italian Salsa Verde. In a bowl, add the finely chopped fresh parsley, chopped capers, minced garlic, olive oil, lemon juice, salt, and pepper. Mix sufficiently to create the salsa.

6. Lay the marinated swordfish steaks in the air fryer basket.

7. Air fry for approximately 8-10 minutes, depending on the thickness of the steaks, until the swordfish is opaque and flakes easily with a fork.

8. Serve the Grilled Swordfish with a generous spoonful of Italian Salsa Verde.

Nutritional Information (per serving):

- Carbs: 4 grams
- Fats: 19 grams
- Fiber: 1 gram
- Protein: 33 grams

Spanish Baked Hake with Tomato and Bell Pepper Sauce

Prep Time: 20 minutes

Cook Time: 15 minutes

Servings: 4

Ingredients:

For the Baked Hake:

- 4 hake fillets (6 ounces each)
- 2 tablespoons olive oil
- Juice of 1 lemon
- 2 cloves garlic, minced
- 1 teaspoon smoked paprika
- Salt and pepper to taste

For the Tomato and Bell Pepper Sauce:

- 2 red bell peppers, diced
- 1 can (14 ounces) diced tomatoes
- 1 onion, diced
- 2 cloves garlic, minced
- 2 tablespoons olive oil
- 1 teaspoon smoked paprika
- Salt and pepper to taste
- Fresh parsley for garnish

Instructions:

1. Preheat your air fryer to 375°F (190°C).

2. In a bowl, add the olive oil, lemon juice, minced garlic, smoked paprika, salt, and pepper. This mixture will be the marinade for the hake.

3. Place the hake fillets in a shallow dish.

4. Pour the marinade over the hake fillets, ensuring evenly coated. Let them marinate for about 10 minutes.

5. In the meantime, prepare the tomato and bell pepper sauce. In a skillet over medium heat, add two tablespoons of olive oil. Sauté the diced onion, diced red bell peppers, and minced garlic until they start to soften, about 5 minutes.

6. Add the diced tomatoes, smoked paprika, salt, and pepper to the skillet. Cook for another 5 minutes, allowing the flavors to meld together.

7. Lay the marinated hake fillets in the air fryer basket.

8. Air fry for approximately 8-10 minutes, depending on the thickness of the fillets, until the hake is opaque and flakes easily with a fork.

9. Serve the Baked Hake with a generous spoonful of the Tomato and Bell Pepper Sauce, garnished with fresh parsley.

Nutritional Information (per serving):

- Carbs: 10 grams
- Fats: 12 grams
- Fiber: 3 grams
- Protein: 25 grams

Lemon Herb Stuffed Trout with Almonds

Prep Time: 20 minutes

Cook Time: 12 minutes

Servings: 4

Ingredients:

For the Stuffed Trout:

- 4 whole trout, gutted and cleaned (about 12 ounces each)
- 1 lemon, thinly sliced
- 4 sprigs fresh rosemary
- 4 cloves garlic, minced
- Salt and pepper to taste

For the Almond Topping:

- 1/2 cup slivered almonds
- 2 tablespoons olive oil
- 2 cloves garlic, minced
- Zest of 1 lemon
- 2 tablespoons fresh parsley, chopped

- Salt and pepper to taste

Instructions:

1. Preheat your air fryer to 375°F (190°C).
2. Prepare the trout for stuffing. Make several diagonal cuts on each side of the trout to allow for even cooking. Season the inside and outside of the trout with salt and pepper.
3. Stuff each trout with lemon slices, a sprig of rosemary, and a portion of minced garlic.
4. Lay the stuffed trout in the air fryer basket.
5. In a skillet over medium heat, add the slivered almonds. Toast them until they turn golden brown, stirring frequently to prevent burning. This should take about 2-3 minutes.
6. Take out the toasted almonds from the skillet and place them in a bowl.
7. In the same skillet, add two tablespoons of olive oil and minced garlic. Sauté the garlic until it becomes fragrant, about 1-2 minutes.
8. Take out the skillet from heat and stir in the lemon zest, chopped fresh parsley, salt, and pepper. This mixture will be the almond topping.
9. Spoon the almond topping evenly over each stuffed trout.
10. Air fry for approximately 10-12 minutes, depending on the size of the trout, until the fish is properly cooked, and the almonds are nicely toasted.
11. Serve the Lemon Herb Stuffed Trout with Almonds hot and enjoy!

Nutritional Information (per serving):

- Carbs: 6 grams
- Fats: 19 grams
- Fiber: 3 grams
- Protein: 32 grams

Greek-style Seafood Paella

Prep Time: 20 minutes

Cook Time: 25 minutes

Servings: 4

Ingredients:

- 1 cup Arborio rice
- 1/2 pound large shrimp, peeled and deveined
- 1/2 pound mussels, cleaned and debearded
- 1/2 pound squid rings and tentacles
- 1/2 cup diced onion
- 1/2 cup diced red bell pepper

- 1/2 cup diced green bell pepper
- 2 cloves garlic, minced
- 2 tablespoons olive oil
- 1 teaspoon smoked paprika
- 1/2 teaspoon saffron threads
- 1/2 teaspoon dried oregano
- 1/4 cup chopped fresh parsley
- 3 cups low-sodium chicken broth
- Salt and pepper to taste
- Lemon wedges for garnish

Instructions:

1. Preheat your air fryer to 375°F (190°C).
2. In a small bowl, add the saffron threads with one tablespoon of warm water. Let them steep and release their color and flavor.
3. In a large skillet, heat the olive oil over medium heat.
4. Add the diced onion and garlic to the skillet and sauté until they become translucent, about 2-3 minutes.
5. Stir in the diced red and green bell peppers, smoked paprika, dried oregano, and saffron with its liquid. Cook for an extra 2-3 minutes until the peppers start to soften.
6. Add the Arborio rice to the skillet and stir to coat the rice with the pepper mixture.
7. Pour in the low-sodium chicken broth and bring the mixture to a simmer. Cover and cook for 15-18 minutes, stirring occasionally, until the rice is tender and most of the liquid is absorbed.
8. While the rice is cooking, lay the shrimp, mussels, and squid rings and tentacles in the air fryer basket.
9. Air fry the seafood for about 3-5 minutes until the shrimp turn pink, the mussels open, and the squid is opaque.
10. Once the rice is cooked and the liquid is mostly absorbed, gently fold in the cooked seafood into the skillet with the rice.
11. Season the Greek-style Seafood Paella with salt and pepper to taste.
12. Garnish with chopped fresh parsley and lemon wedges before serving.

Nutritional Information (per serving):

- Carbs: 54 grams
- Fats: 9 grams
- Fiber: 2 grams
- Protein: 30 grams

Moroccan Spiced Scallops with Roasted Red Pepper Sauce

Prep Time: 15 minutes

Cook Time: 10 minutes

Servings: 4

Ingredients:

For the Spiced Scallops:

- 16 large scallops
- 1 teaspoon ground cumin
- 1 teaspoon ground coriander
- 1/2 teaspoon ground paprika
- 1/2 teaspoon ground cinnamon
- Salt and pepper to taste
- 2 tablespoons olive oil
- Juice of 1 lemon

For the Roasted Red Pepper Sauce:

- 2 red bell peppers, roasted, peeled, and seeded
- 2 cloves garlic, minced
- 1/2 cup low-sodium chicken broth
- 1 teaspoon ground cumin
- 1/2 teaspoon ground coriander
- Salt and pepper to taste
- Fresh cilantro leaves for garnish

Instructions:

1. Preheat your air fryer to 375°F (190°C).
2. In a bowl, add the ground cumin, ground coriander, ground paprika, ground cinnamon, salt, and pepper. This mixture will be the spice rub for the scallops.
3. Pat the scallops dry with a paper towel, then coat them with the spice rub, ensuring evenly seasoned.
4. Lay the seasoned scallops in the air fryer basket.
5. Air fry for approximately 4-5 minutes on each side, until the scallops are opaque and lightly browned.
6. While the scallops are cooking, prepare the roasted red pepper sauce. In a blender, add the roasted red peppers, minced garlic, low-sodium chicken broth, ground cumin, ground coriander, salt, and pepper. Blend until smooth.
7. Pour the roasted red pepper sauce into a saucepan and warm it over low heat, stirring occasionally.
8. Once the scallops are done, take them out from the air fryer.
9. Serve the Moroccan Spiced Scallops with a drizzle of the roasted red pepper sauce and garnish with fresh cilantro leaves.

Nutritional Information (per serving):

- Carbs: 9 grams
- Fats: 9 grams
- Fiber: 2 grams
- Protein: 25 grams

POULTRY

Mediterranean Chicken Shawarma

Prep Time: 15 minutes

Cook Time: 20 minutes

Servings: 4

Ingredients:

- 1 pound boneless, skinless chicken thighs
- 2 tablespoons olive oil
- 2 cloves garlic, minced
- 1 teaspoon ground cumin
- 1 teaspoon ground paprika
- 1 teaspoon ground coriander
- 1/2 teaspoon ground turmeric
- 1/2 teaspoon ground cinnamon
- 1/4 teaspoon cayenne pepper
- Salt and black pepper to taste
- 1 medium red onion, thinly sliced
- 1 medium red bell pepper, thinly sliced
- 1 medium yellow bell pepper, thinly sliced
- 1 medium green bell pepper, thinly sliced
- 4 whole wheat pita bread rounds
- Tzatziki sauce or yogurt for serving
- Fresh parsley leaves for garnish

Instructions:

1. In a bowl, add the olive oil, minced garlic, ground cumin, ground paprika, ground coriander, ground turmeric, ground cinnamon, cayenne pepper, salt, and black pepper. Mix sufficiently to create a marinade.

2. Cut the boneless, skinless chicken thighs into thin strips. Add the chicken strips to the marinade and coat them evenly. Allow the chicken to marinate for at least 10 minutes, or refrigerate for a more extended period for enhanced flavor.

3. Preheat your air fryer to 375°F (190°C).

4. Place the marinated chicken strips in a single layer in the air fryer basket. Cook for 10-12 minutes or until the chicken is properly cooked and has a slightly charred appearance, flipping halfway through the cooking time for even browning.

5. While the chicken is cooking, heat a non-stick skillet over medium heat. Add a drizzle of olive oil and sauté the sliced red onion and bell peppers until tender and slightly caramelized, about 5-7 minutes. Season with a pinch of salt and black pepper.

6. Warm the whole wheat pita bread rounds in the air fryer for 1-2 minutes until slightly toasted.

7. To assemble the Mediterranean Chicken Shawarma wraps, spread a spoonful of tzatziki sauce or yogurt on each pita bread round. Top with the cooked chicken strips and the sautéed onion and bell peppers.

8. Garnish with fresh parsley leaves and fold the pita bread in half. Serve immediately.

Nutritional Information (per serving):

- Carbs: 42 grams
- Fats: 15 grams
- Fiber: 7 grams
- Protein: 29 grams

Lemon Oregano Turkey Meatballs

Prep Time: 15 minutes

Cook Time: 12 minutes

Servings: 4

Ingredients:

- 1 pound lean ground turkey
- 1/4 cup whole wheat breadcrumbs
- 1/4 cup finely grated Parmesan cheese
- 1/4 cup finely chopped fresh parsley
- 1/4 cup finely chopped red onion
- 2 cloves garlic, minced
- 1 large egg
- Zest of 1 lemon
- 1 tablespoon fresh lemon juice
- 1 teaspoon dried oregano
- Salt and black pepper to taste
- Olive oil cooking spray

Instructions:

1. In a large mixing bowl, add the lean ground turkey, whole wheat breadcrumbs, finely grated Parmesan cheese, finely chopped fresh parsley, finely chopped red onion, minced garlic, large egg, lemon zest, lemon juice, dried oregano, salt, and black pepper.

2. Mix all the ingredients until well combined.

3. Preheat your air fryer to 375°F (190°C).

4. Using clean hands, shape the turkey mixture into meatballs, approximately 1.5 inches in diameter. This should yield about 16 meatballs.

5. Lightly spray the air fryer basket with olive oil cooking spray to prevent sticking.

6. Place the turkey meatballs in a single layer in the air fryer basket, ensuring not touching.

7. Cook the meatballs in the air fryer for 10-12 minutes, or until properly cooked and have a golden-brown exterior. Be sure to turn them halfway through the cooking time for even browning.

8. Once cooked, take out the meatballs from the air fryer and let them cool slightly before serving.

Nutritional Information (per serving):

- Carbs: 9 grams
- Fats: 8 grams
- Fiber: 1 gram
- Protein: 27 grams

Moroccan Spiced Chicken Tagine

Prep Time: 15 minutes

Cook Time: 20 minutes

Servings: 4

Ingredients:

- 1 pound boneless, skinless chicken breasts, cut into 1-inch cubes
- 1 onion, finely chopped
- 2 cloves garlic, minced
- 1 teaspoon ground cumin
- 1 teaspoon ground coriander
- 1 teaspoon ground paprika
- 1/2 teaspoon ground cinnamon
- 1/2 teaspoon ground ginger
- 1/4 teaspoon cayenne pepper (adjust to taste)
- 1 can (14 ounces) diced tomatoes, drained
- 1/2 cup low-sodium chicken broth
- 1/4 cup chopped dried apricots
- 1/4 cup chopped almonds
- 1 tablespoon olive oil
- Salt and black pepper to taste
- Fresh cilantro leaves for garnish
- Cooked quinoa or couscous for serving (optional)

Instructions:

1. In a large bowl, add the boneless, skinless chicken breast cubes, ground cumin, ground coriander, ground

paprika, ground cinnamon, ground ginger, cayenne pepper, salt, and black pepper. Toss the chicken pieces to coat them evenly with the spices.

2. Preheat your air fryer to 375°F (190°C).

3. Heat olive oil in a skillet over medium heat. Add the finely chopped onion and minced garlic. Sauté for 2-3 minutes or until the onions become translucent.

4. Add the spiced chicken pieces to the skillet and cook for about 5 minutes, or until the chicken is lightly browned on all sides.

5. Transfer the cooked chicken and onion mixture to the air fryer basket.

6. Add the drained diced tomatoes, low-sodium chicken broth, and chopped dried apricots to the air fryer basket with the chicken.

7. Cook the tagine mixture in the air fryer for 10-12 minutes, stirring occasionally until the chicken is properly cooked, and the sauce thickens slightly.

8. While the tagine is cooking, toast the chopped almonds in a dry skillet over medium heat until lightly browned and fragrant. Set them aside.

9. Serve the Moroccan Spiced Chicken Tagine over cooked quinoa or couscous if desired, and garnish with chopped almonds and fresh cilantro leaves.

Nutritional Information (per serving):

- Carbs: 18 grams
- Fats: 9 grams
- Fiber: 4 grams
- Protein: 29 grams

Grilled Harissa Chicken Thighs

Prep Time: 15 minutes

Cook Time: 15 minutes

Servings: 4

Ingredients:

- 4 boneless, skinless chicken thighs
- 2 tablespoons harissa paste
- 1 tablespoon olive oil
- 2 cloves garlic, minced
- 1 teaspoon ground cumin
- 1 teaspoon ground coriander
- 1/2 teaspoon smoked paprika
- Salt and black pepper to taste
- Lemon wedges for serving
- Fresh cilantro leaves for garnish

Instructions:

1. In a bowl, add the harissa paste, olive oil, minced garlic, ground cumin, ground coriander, smoked paprika, salt, and black pepper. Mix sufficiently to create a marinade.

2. Place the boneless, skinless chicken thighs in a resealable plastic bag or shallow dish. Pour the harissa marinade over the chicken thighs, ensuring evenly coated. Seal the bag or cover the dish and refrigerate for at least 15 minutes, or longer for better flavor.

3. Preheat your air fryer to 375°F (190°C).

4. Take out the marinated chicken thighs from the bag or dish and place them in the air fryer basket in a single layer.

5. Cook the chicken thighs in the air fryer for 12-15 minutes, flipping halfway through the cooking time, or until the chicken reaches an internal temperature of 165°F (74°C) and is nicely charred on the outside.

6. Once cooked, transfer the grilled harissa chicken thighs to a serving platter.

7. Garnish with fresh cilantro leaves and serve with lemon wedges for added flavor.

Nutritional Information (per serving):

- Carbs: 2 grams
- Fats: 9 grams
- Fiber: 0 grams
- Protein: 27 grams

Spinach and Feta Stuffed Chicken Breast

Prep Time: 20 minutes

Cook Time: 20 minutes

Servings: 4

Ingredients:

- 4 boneless, skinless chicken breasts
- 2 cups fresh spinach, chopped
- 1/2 cup crumbled feta cheese
- 1/4 cup low-fat Greek yogurt
- 2 cloves garlic, minced
- 1/2 teaspoon dried oregano
- 1/2 teaspoon dried basil
- Salt and black pepper to taste
- Olive oil cooking spray

Instructions:

1. In a bowl, add the chopped fresh spinach, crumbled feta cheese, low-fat Greek yogurt, minced garlic, dried oregano, dried basil, salt, and black pepper. Mix

sufficiently to create the stuffing mixture.

2. Preheat your air fryer to 375°F (190°C).

3. Lay each chicken breast flat on a clean surface. Using a sharp knife, make a horizontal slit in the thickest part of each chicken breast, creating a pocket without cutting all the way through.

4. Stuff each chicken breast with the spinach and feta mixture, dividing it evenly among the four breasts. Press the edges of the chicken to seal the pockets.

5. Lightly spray the air fryer basket with olive oil cooking spray.

6. Place the stuffed chicken breasts in the air fryer basket, ensuring not touching.

7. Cook the chicken in the air fryer for 18-20 minutes, or until the chicken is properly cooked and the internal temperature reaches 165°F (74°C).

8. Serve the Spinach and Feta Stuffed Chicken Breast hot, garnished with additional fresh herbs if desired.

Nutritional Information (per serving):

- Carbs: 4 grams
- Fats: 9 grams
- Fiber: 1 gram
- Protein: 38 grams

Lemon Rosemary Grilled Turkey Breast

Prep Time: 15 minutes

Cook Time: 20 minutes

Servings: 4

Ingredients:

- 4 boneless, skinless turkey breast fillets
- Zest of 1 lemon
- Juice of 1 lemon
- 2 tablespoons olive oil
- 2 cloves garlic, minced
- 2 teaspoons fresh rosemary leaves, finely chopped
- Salt and black pepper to taste
- Lemon wedges for serving
- Fresh rosemary sprigs for garnish

Instructions:

1. In a bowl, add the lemon zest, lemon juice, olive oil, minced garlic, finely chopped fresh rosemary leaves, salt, and black pepper. Mix sufficiently to create a marinade.

2. Place the boneless, skinless turkey breast fillets in a resealable plastic bag or shallow dish. Pour the lemon

rosemary marinade over the turkey fillets, ensuring evenly coated. Seal the bag or cover the dish and refrigerate for at least 15 minutes to marinate.

3. Preheat your air fryer to 375°F (190°C).

4. Take out the marinated turkey breast fillets from the bag or dish and place them in the air fryer basket in a single layer.

5. Cook the turkey fillets in the air fryer for 18-20 minutes, flipping them halfway through the cooking time, or until the turkey is properly cooked and reaches an internal temperature of 165°F (74°C).

6. Once cooked, transfer the grilled lemon rosemary turkey breast fillets to a serving platter.

7. Garnish with lemon wedges and fresh rosemary sprigs for added flavor and presentation.

Nutritional Information (per serving):

- Carbs: 2 grams
- Fats: 6 grams
- Fiber: 0 grams
- Protein: 32 grams

Mediterranean Chicken and Artichoke Skewers

Prep Time: 20 minutes

Cook Time: 15 minutes

Servings: 4

Ingredients:

- 1 pound boneless, skinless chicken breasts, cut into 1-inch cubes
- 1 can (14 ounces) artichoke hearts, drained and halved
- 1 red bell pepper, cut into 1-inch pieces
- 1 yellow bell pepper, cut into 1-inch pieces
- 1 red onion, cut into 1-inch pieces
- 2 cloves garlic, minced
- 2 tablespoons olive oil
- 1 teaspoon dried oregano
- 1 teaspoon dried basil
- Salt and black pepper to taste
- Lemon wedges for serving
- Fresh parsley leaves for garnish

Instructions:

1. In a large bowl, add the boneless, skinless chicken breast cubes, halved artichoke hearts, red bell pepper pieces, yellow bell pepper pieces, red onion pieces, minced garlic, olive oil, dried oregano, dried

basil, salt, and black pepper. Toss well to coat all the ingredients in the marinade.

2. Preheat your air fryer to 375°F (190°C).
3. Thread the marinated chicken, artichoke hearts, bell pepper pieces, and red onion pieces onto skewers, alternating the ingredients as desired.
4. Lightly spray the air fryer basket with olive oil cooking spray.
5. Place the chicken and artichoke skewers in the air fryer basket in a single layer.
6. Cook the skewers in the air fryer for 12-15 minutes, turning them halfway through the cooking time, or until the chicken is properly cooked and the vegetables are tender.
7. Once cooked, take out the Mediterranean Chicken and Artichoke Skewers from the air fryer.
8. Serve the skewers hot, garnished with lemon wedges and fresh parsley leaves for added flavor and presentation.

Nutritional Information (per serving):

- Carbs: 14 grams
- Fats: 10 grams
- Fiber: 6 grams
- Protein: 29 grams

Moroccan Chicken with Apricots and Almonds

Prep Time: 20 minutes

Cook Time: 25 minutes

Servings: 4

Ingredients:

- 4 bone-in, skinless chicken thighs
- 1/2 cup dried apricots, chopped
- 1/4 cup slivered almonds
- 1 onion, finely chopped
- 2 cloves garlic, minced
- 1 teaspoon ground cumin
- 1 teaspoon ground coriander
- 1/2 teaspoon ground cinnamon
- 1/2 teaspoon ground ginger
- 1/4 teaspoon cayenne pepper
- 1 can (14 ounces) diced tomatoes, undrained
- 1/2 cup low-sodium chicken broth
- Salt and black pepper to taste
- Fresh cilantro leaves for garnish

Instructions:

1. Preheat your air fryer to 375°F (190°C).

2. In a large bowl, add the dried apricots and slivered almonds. Set aside.

3. Heat a non-stick skillet over medium heat. Add the finely chopped onion and minced garlic. Sauté for 2-3 minutes, or until the onions become translucent.

4. Add the bone-in, skinless chicken thighs to the skillet and cook for about 5 minutes on each side, or until lightly browned. Take out the chicken from the skillet and set aside.

5. In the same skillet, add the ground cumin, ground coriander, ground cinnamon, ground ginger, and cayenne pepper. Stir for about 1 minute until fragrant.

6. Return the chicken thighs to the skillet and add the diced tomatoes (with their juices) and low-sodium chicken broth. Season with salt and black pepper to taste. Bring the mixture to a simmer.

7. Transfer the chicken and tomato mixture to the air fryer basket.

8. Cook in the air fryer for 20-25 minutes, or until the chicken is properly cooked, and the sauce has thickened, stirring occasionally.

9. During the last 5 minutes of cooking, add the apricots and almonds mixture to the air fryer basket and cook until the apricots are softened, and the almonds are toasted.

10. Serve the Moroccan Chicken with Apricots and Almonds hot, garnished with fresh cilantro leaves.

Nutritional Information (per serving):

- Carbs: 21 grams
- Fats: 15 grams
- Fiber: 4 grams
- Protein: 31 grams

Greek Lemon Garlic Chicken with Green Beans

Prep Time: 15 minutes

Cook Time: 20 minutes

Servings: 4

Ingredients:

- 4 boneless, skinless chicken breasts
- 1 pound fresh green beans, trimmed
- 4 cloves garlic, minced
- Zest of 1 lemon
- Juice of 1 lemon
- 2 tablespoons olive oil
- 1 teaspoon dried oregano

- 1/2 teaspoon dried thyme
- Salt and black pepper to taste
- Lemon wedges for serving
- Fresh parsley leaves for garnish

Instructions:

1. In a bowl, add the minced garlic, lemon zest, lemon juice, olive oil, dried oregano, dried thyme, salt, and black pepper. Mix sufficiently to create a marinade.
2. Place the boneless, skinless chicken breasts in a resealable plastic bag or shallow dish. Pour the lemon garlic marinade over the chicken breasts, ensuring evenly coated. Seal the bag or cover the dish and refrigerate for at least 15 minutes to marinate.
3. Preheat your air fryer to 375°F (190°C).
4. Take out the marinated chicken breasts from the bag or dish and place them in the air fryer basket in a single layer.
5. Cook the chicken breasts in the air fryer for 15-18 minutes, or until the chicken is properly cooked and reaches an internal temperature of 165°F (74°C).
6. While the chicken is cooking, lightly spray the air fryer basket with olive oil cooking spray and add the trimmed fresh green beans.
7. Cook the green beans in the air fryer for 10-12 minutes or until tender and slightly browned.
8. Once cooked, transfer the Greek Lemon Garlic Chicken and green beans to a serving platter.
9. Garnish with lemon wedges and fresh parsley leaves for added flavor and presentation.

Nutritional Information (per serving):

- Carbs: 12 grams
- Fats: 10 grams
- Fiber: 4 grams
- Protein: 35 grams

Harissa Roasted Quail with Mint Yogurt Sauce

Prep Time: 15 minutes

Cook Time: 15 minutes

Servings: 4

Ingredients:

For the Quail:

- 8 whole quail, cleaned and butterflied
- 2 tablespoons harissa paste
- 2 tablespoons olive oil

- 2 cloves garlic, minced
- 1 teaspoon ground cumin
- 1 teaspoon ground coriander
- 1/2 teaspoon smoked paprika
- Salt and black pepper to taste

For the Mint Yogurt Sauce:
- 1 cup low-fat Greek yogurt
- 2 tablespoons fresh mint leaves, finely chopped
- 1 clove garlic, minced
- 1 tablespoon lemon juice
- Salt and black pepper to taste

Instructions:

1. In a bowl, add the harissa paste, olive oil, minced garlic, ground cumin, ground coriander, smoked paprika, salt, and black pepper. Mix sufficiently to create a marinade.
2. Place the butterflied quail in a resealable plastic bag or shallow dish. Pour the harissa marinade over the quail, ensuring evenly coated. Seal the bag or cover the dish and refrigerate for at least 15 minutes to marinate.
3. Preheat your air fryer to 375°F (190°C).
4. Take out the marinated quail from the bag or dish and place them in the air fryer basket in a single layer.
5. Cook the quail in the air fryer for 12-15 minutes, turning them halfway through the cooking time, or until the quail is properly cooked and has a nicely charred exterior.
6. While the quail is cooking, prepare the mint yogurt sauce. In a bowl, add the low-fat Greek yogurt, finely chopped fresh mint leaves, minced garlic, lemon juice, salt, and black pepper. Mix sufficiently and refrigerate until ready to serve.
7. Once cooked, transfer the Harissa Roasted Quail to a serving platter.
8. Serve the quail hot with the mint yogurt sauce on the side for dipping.

Nutritional Information (per serving):
- Carbs: 4 grams
- Fats: 6 grams
- Fiber: 0 grams
- Protein: 28 grams

Italian Herb Roasted Turkey Cutlets

Prep Time: 15 minutes
Cook Time: 12 minutes
Number of Servings: 4

Ingredients:
- 1 pound (16 ounces) turkey cutlets

- 2 tablespoons olive oil
- 2 teaspoons dried basil
- 2 teaspoons dried oregano
- 2 teaspoons dried rosemary
- 1 teaspoon dried thyme
- 1 teaspoon garlic powder
- 1 teaspoon onion powder
- 1/2 teaspoon salt
- 1/4 teaspoon black pepper
- 1 lemon, juiced and zested
- 2 tablespoons fresh parsley, chopped

Instructions:

1. In a small bowl, mix together the dried basil, dried oregano, dried rosemary, dried thyme, garlic powder, onion powder, salt, and black pepper.
2. Rub the herb mixture evenly over both sides of the turkey cutlets.
3. Preheat your Air Fryer to 375°F (190°C).
4. Brush the turkey cutlets with olive oil on both sides.
5. Place the turkey cutlets in a single layer in the Air Fryer basket, ensuring not overlapping.
6. Cook in the Air Fryer at 375°F (190°C) for 6 minutes, then flip the turkey cutlets and cook for an extra 6 minutes or until they reach an internal temperature of 165°F (74°C).
7. While the turkey is cooking, prepare the lemon zest and juice from the lemon.
8. Once the turkey cutlets are done, take them out from the Air Fryer and drizzle with the fresh lemon juice and sprinkle with lemon zest.
9. Garnish with fresh chopped parsley.
10. Serve hot and enjoy your Mediterranean-style Italian Herb Roasted Turkey Cutlets!

Nutritional Information (per serving):

- Carbs: 2 grams
- Fats: 7 grams
- Fiber: 1 gram
- Protein: 29 grams

Greek Lemon Rosemary Chicken Thighs

Prep Time: 15 minutes
Cook Time: 20 minutes
Number of Servings: 4

Ingredients:

- 4 boneless, skinless chicken thighs (about 1.5 pounds)
- 2 tablespoons olive oil
- 2 tablespoons fresh rosemary leaves, chopped

- 2 cloves garlic, minced
- 1 lemon, juiced and zested
- 1 teaspoon dried oregano
- 1/2 teaspoon salt
- 1/4 teaspoon black pepper

Instructions:

1. In a bowl, add the olive oil, chopped fresh rosemary, minced garlic, lemon juice, lemon zest, dried oregano, salt, and black pepper.
2. Place the chicken thighs in a resealable plastic bag or a shallow dish and pour the marinade over them.
3. Seal the bag or cover the dish and refrigerate for at least 30 minutes to marinate. You can also marinate it for a few hours or overnight for enhanced flavor.
4. Preheat your Air Fryer to 375°F (190°C).
5. Take out the chicken thighs from the marinade, allowing any excess to drip off.
6. Place the chicken thighs in the Air Fryer basket in a single layer, ensuring not overcrowded.
7. Cook in the Air Fryer at 375°F (190°C) for about 20 minutes or until the chicken thighs reach an internal temperature of 165°F (74°C) and the exterior is crispy and browned.
8. While the chicken is cooking, you can prepare a side salad or veggies to accompany your meal.
9. Once cooked, take out the chicken thighs from the Air Fryer.
10. Serve hot, garnished with additional fresh rosemary if desired.

Nutritional Information (per serving):

- Carbs: 2 grams
- Fats: 12 grams
- Fiber: 1 gram
- Protein: 27 grams

Moroccan Chicken and Olive Tagine

Prep Time: 20 minutes
Cook Time: 30 minutes
Number of Servings: 4

Ingredients:

- 4 boneless, skinless chicken thighs (about 1.5 pounds)
- 1 tablespoon olive oil
- 1 onion, finely chopped
- 2 cloves garlic, minced
- 1 teaspoon ground cumin
- 1 teaspoon ground coriander
- 1 teaspoon ground paprika
- 1/2 teaspoon ground cinnamon

- 1/2 teaspoon ground ginger
- 1/2 teaspoon ground turmeric
- 1/4 teaspoon cayenne pepper (adjust to taste)
- 1 can (14 ounces) diced tomatoes, undrained
- 1/2 cup chicken broth
- 1 cup green olives, pitted
- 2 tablespoons fresh cilantro, chopped
- Salt and black pepper to taste

Instructions:

1. In a large bowl, mix together the ground cumin, ground coriander, ground paprika, ground cinnamon, ground ginger, ground turmeric, and cayenne pepper.
2. Season the chicken thighs with this spice mixture, ensuring well coated. Let them marinate for about 10 minutes.
3. Preheat your Air Fryer to 375°F (190°C).
4. In a large skillet, heat the olive oil over medium heat. Add the chopped onion and minced garlic, sautéing until they become soft and translucent.
5. Add the marinated chicken thighs to the skillet and cook for about 2-3 minutes on each side until lightly browned.
6. Stir in the diced tomatoes (with their juices) and chicken broth. Season with salt and black pepper to taste. Simmer for about 5 minutes until the sauce thickens slightly.
7. Transfer the chicken and tomato mixture to the Air Fryer basket.
8. Add the green olives on top of the chicken.
9. Cook in the Air Fryer at 375°F (190°C) for approximately 20 minutes or until the chicken thighs are properly cooked and reach an internal temperature of 165°F (74°C).
10. Garnish with fresh chopped cilantro before serving.
11. Serve hot and enjoy your Mediterranean-inspired Moroccan Chicken and Olive Tagine!

Nutritional Information (per serving):

- Carbs: 10 grams
- Fats: 14 grams
- Fiber: 3 grams
- Protein: 29 grams

Lemon Garlic Turkey and Vegetable Skewers

Prep Time: 20 minutes
Cook Time: 15 minutes
Number of Servings: 4

Ingredients:

- 1 pound (16 ounces) turkey breast, cut into 1-inch cubes
- 2 zucchinis, sliced into 1/2-inch rounds
- 1 red bell pepper, cut into 1-inch squares
- 1 yellow bell pepper, cut into 1-inch squares
- 1 red onion, cut into 1-inch wedges
- 2 tablespoons olive oil
- 2 cloves garlic, minced
- 1 lemon, juiced and zested
- 1 teaspoon dried oregano
- 1/2 teaspoon salt
- 1/4 teaspoon black pepper
- Wooden skewers, soaked in water for 30 minutes to prevent burning

Instructions:

1. In a bowl, whisk the olive oil, minced garlic, lemon juice, lemon zest, dried oregano, salt, and black pepper to create the marinade.
2. Place the turkey breast cubes in a resealable plastic bag or a shallow dish and pour the marinade over them. Ensure the turkey is evenly coated. Marinate for at least 15 minutes, or you can refrigerate it for a few hours for better flavor.
3. Preheat your Air Fryer to 375°F (190°C).
4. While the turkey is marinating, assemble your skewers by alternating the marinated turkey cubes with the sliced zucchini, red bell pepper, yellow bell pepper, and red onion wedges.
5. Place the assembled skewers in the Air Fryer basket, ensuring not overcrowded.
6. Cook in the Air Fryer at 375°F (190°C) for approximately 12-15 minutes, turning the skewers halfway through the cooking time. Cook until the turkey is fully cooked and the vegetables are tender and slightly charred.
7. While the skewers are cooking, you can prepare a simple side salad or sauce for dipping, if desired.
8. Once done, take out the skewers from the Air Fryer.
9. Serve hot, and enjoy your healthy Mediterranean Lemon Garlic Turkey and Vegetable Skewers!

Nutritional Information (per serving):

- Carbs: 11 grams
- Fats: 7 grams
- Fiber: 3 grams
- Protein: 32 grams

Tuscan Herb Stuffed Quail

Prep Time: 30 minutes
Cook Time: 20 minutes
Number of Servings: 4

Ingredients:

- 4 whole quail, cleaned and deboned
- 1 cup fresh spinach, chopped
- 1/2 cup sun-dried tomatoes, chopped
- 1/4 cup fresh basil leaves, chopped
- 2 cloves garlic, minced
- 2 tablespoons olive oil
- 1 teaspoon dried oregano
- 1 teaspoon dried rosemary
- 1/2 teaspoon dried thyme
- 1/2 teaspoon dried sage
- 1/2 teaspoon salt
- 1/4 teaspoon black pepper
- 1 lemon, juiced and zested
- Wooden toothpicks, for securing

Instructions:

1. In a skillet, heat one tablespoon of olive oil over medium heat. Add the minced garlic and cook for about 30 seconds until fragrant.
2. Add the chopped fresh spinach, sun-dried tomatoes, and fresh basil to the skillet. Sauté for 2-3 minutes until the spinach wilts and the ingredients are well combined. Take it out from heat and set aside.
3. In a small bowl, mix together the dried oregano, dried rosemary, dried thyme, dried sage, salt, and black pepper.
4. Season the deboned quail with the herb mixture, ensuring to coat both the inside and outside of each quail.
5. Stuff each quail with the sautéed spinach and tomato mixture.
6. Use wooden toothpicks to secure the quail openings and keep the stuffing in place.
7. Preheat your Air Fryer to 375°F (190°C).
8. Brush the stuffed quail with the remaining one tablespoon of olive oil and place them in the Air Fryer basket, ensuring not overcrowded.
9. Cook in the Air Fryer at 375°F (190°C) for

approximately 18-20 minutes or until the quail are properly cooked and have a golden brown exterior.

10. While the quail is cooking, prepare a simple sauce by mixing the lemon juice and zest.

11. Once done, take out the quail from the Air Fryer and drizzle them with the lemon sauce.

12. Serve hot, and savor the flavors of your Mediterranean-inspired Tuscan Herb Stuffed Quail!

Nutritional Information (per serving):

- Carbs: 8 grams
- Fats: 11 grams
- Fiber: 2 grams
- Protein: 21 grams

Italian Herbed Turkey Meatloaf with Roasted Vegetables

Prep Time: 20 minutes
Cook Time: 30 minutes
Number of Servings: 4

Ingredients:

For the Turkey Meatloaf:

- 1 pound (16 ounces) ground turkey
- 1/2 cup breadcrumbs
- 1/4 cup grated Parmesan cheese
- 1/4 cup fresh parsley, chopped
- 2 cloves garlic, minced
- 1 egg
- 1 teaspoon dried oregano
- 1 teaspoon dried basil
- 1/2 teaspoon dried thyme
- 1/2 teaspoon dried rosemary
- 1/2 teaspoon salt
- 1/4 teaspoon black pepper

For the Roasted Vegetables:

- 2 cups mixed Mediterranean vegetables (e.g., bell peppers, zucchini, cherry tomatoes)
- 2 tablespoons olive oil
- 1 teaspoon dried oregano
- 1/2 teaspoon dried basil
- 1/2 teaspoon dried thyme
- 1/2 teaspoon dried rosemary
- 1/2 teaspoon salt
- 1/4 teaspoon black pepper

Instructions:

1. In a large bowl, add the ground turkey, breadcrumbs, grated Parmesan cheese, chopped fresh parsley, minced garlic, egg, dried oregano, dried basil, dried thyme, dried rosemary, salt, and black

pepper. Mix until well combined.

2. Preheat your Air Fryer to 375°F (190°C).

3. Form the turkey mixture into a loaf shape and place it in the Air Fryer basket.

4. In a separate bowl, toss the mixed Mediterranean vegetables with olive oil, dried oregano, dried basil, dried thyme, dried rosemary, salt, and black pepper.

5. Arrange the seasoned vegetables around the turkey meatloaf in the Air Fryer basket.

6. Cook in the Air Fryer at 375°F (190°C) for approximately 25-30 minutes or until the turkey meatloaf is properly cooked and reaches an internal temperature of 165°F (74°C) and the vegetables are tender.

7. While the meatloaf and vegetables are cooking, you can prepare a simple tomato sauce or yogurt-based sauce for serving, if desired.

8. Once done, take out the turkey meatloaf and roasted vegetables from the Air Fryer.

9. Slice the turkey meatloaf and serve it with the roasted Mediterranean vegetables.

Nutritional Information (per serving):

- Carbs: 22 grams
- Fats: 16 grams
- Fiber: 4 grams
- Protein: 36 grams

Lemon Rosemary Chicken and Quinoa Bowls

Prep Time: 15 minutes
Cook Time: 20 minutes
Number of Servings: 4

Ingredients:

For the Lemon Rosemary Chicken:

- 4 boneless, skinless chicken breasts (about 1.5 pounds)
- 2 tablespoons olive oil
- 2 tablespoons fresh rosemary leaves, chopped
- 2 cloves garlic, minced
- 1 lemon, juiced and zested
- 1/2 teaspoon salt
- 1/4 teaspoon black pepper

For the Quinoa Bowls:

- 1 cup quinoa
- 2 cups water
- 2 cups mixed Mediterranean vegetables (e.g., bell peppers, zucchini, cherry tomatoes), diced
- 1 tablespoon olive oil

- 1 teaspoon dried oregano
- 1/2 teaspoon dried thyme
- 1/2 teaspoon dried rosemary
- Salt and black pepper to taste
- Fresh parsley, chopped (for garnish)

Instructions:

For the Lemon Rosemary Chicken:

1. In a bowl, mix together the olive oil, chopped fresh rosemary, minced garlic, lemon juice, lemon zest, salt, and black pepper to create the marinade.
2. Place the chicken breasts in a resealable plastic bag or a shallow dish and pour the marinade over them. Ensure the chicken is well coated. Marinate for at least 15 minutes.
3. Preheat your Air Fryer to 375°F (190°C).
4. Take out the chicken breasts from the marinade, allowing any excess to drip off.
5. Place the chicken breasts in the Air Fryer basket and cook at 375°F (190°C) for about 18-20 minutes or until they reach an internal temperature of 165°F (74°C) and have a golden brown exterior. Turn the chicken breasts halfway through the cooking time for even cooking.

For the Quinoa Bowls:

1. Rinse the quinoa under cold water using a fine-mesh strainer.
2. In a medium saucepan, add the rinsed quinoa and two cups of water. Bring to a boil, then reduce the heat to low, cover, and simmer for about 15 minutes or until the quinoa is cooked and the water is absorbed. Fluff the quinoa with a fork.
3. While the quinoa is cooking, toss the diced Mediterranean vegetables with olive oil, dried oregano, dried thyme, dried rosemary, salt, and black pepper.
4. Preheat your Air Fryer to 375°F (190°C).
5. Place the seasoned vegetables in the Air Fryer basket and cook at 375°F (190°C) for about 10-12 minutes or until tender and slightly charred.

Assembly:

1. Divide the cooked quinoa among four bowls.
2. Slice the cooked Lemon Rosemary Chicken breasts and place them on top of the quinoa.
3. Add the roasted Mediterranean vegetables to each bowl.

4. Garnish with chopped fresh parsley.
5. Serve hot and enjoy your weight-loss-friendly Mediterranean Lemon Rosemary Chicken and Quinoa Bowls!

Nutritional Information (per serving):

- Carbs: 40 grams
- Fats: 12 grams
- Fiber: 6 grams
- Protein: 32 grams

Greek Lemon Garlic Turkey Cutlets with Tzatziki

Prep Time: 15 minutes
Cook Time: 12 minutes
Number of Servings: 4

Ingredients:

For the Greek Lemon Garlic Turkey Cutlets:

- 4 turkey cutlets (about 1.5 pounds)
- 2 tablespoons olive oil
- 2 cloves garlic, minced
- 1 lemon, juiced and zested
- 1 teaspoon dried oregano
- 1/2 teaspoon dried thyme
- 1/2 teaspoon dried rosemary
- 1/2 teaspoon dried basil
- 1/2 teaspoon salt
- 1/4 teaspoon black pepper

For the Tzatziki Sauce:

- 1 cup Greek yogurt
- 1/2 cucumber, grated and squeezed to remove excess moisture
- 2 cloves garlic, minced
- 1 tablespoon fresh dill, chopped
- 1 tablespoon fresh mint, chopped
- 1 tablespoon lemon juice
- Salt and black pepper to taste

Instructions:

For the Greek Lemon Garlic Turkey Cutlets:

1. In a bowl, mix together the olive oil, minced garlic, lemon juice, lemon zest, dried oregano, dried thyme, dried rosemary, dried basil, salt, and black pepper to create the marinade.
2. Place the turkey cutlets in a resealable plastic bag or a shallow dish and pour the marinade over them. Ensure the turkey is well coated. Marinate for at least 15 minutes.
3. Preheat your Air Fryer to 375°F (190°C).
4. Take out the turkey cutlets from the marinade, allowing any excess to drip off.

5. Place the turkey cutlets in the Air Fryer basket and cook at 375°F (190°C) for about 6 minutes on each side, or until they reach an internal temperature of 165°F (74°C) and have a golden brown exterior.

For the Tzatziki Sauce:

1. In a bowl, add the Greek yogurt, grated cucumber, minced garlic, chopped fresh dill, chopped fresh mint, and lemon juice. Mix sufficiently.

2. Season the Tzatziki sauce with salt and black pepper to taste. Adjust the seasonings to your preference.

Assembly:

1. Serve the cooked Greek Lemon Garlic Turkey Cutlets hot, accompanied by a generous dollop of Tzatziki sauce on top or on the side.

2. Optionally, garnish with additional fresh herbs or lemon slices.

3. Enjoy your weight-loss-friendly Mediterranean-inspired Greek meal!

Nutritional Information (per serving):

- Carbs: 7 grams
- Fats: 11 grams
- Fiber: 1 gram
- Protein: 38 grams

Moroccan Spiced Chicken Skewers with Yogurt-Harissa Dip

Prep Time: 20 minutes
Cook Time: 15 minutes
Number of Servings: 4

Ingredients:

For the Moroccan Spiced Chicken Skewers:

- 1 pound (16 ounces) boneless, skinless chicken breasts, cut into 1-inch cubes
- 2 tablespoons olive oil
- 1 teaspoon ground cumin
- 1 teaspoon ground coriander
- 1 teaspoon smoked paprika
- 1/2 teaspoon ground cinnamon
- 1/2 teaspoon ground ginger
- 1/2 teaspoon ground turmeric
- 1/4 teaspoon cayenne pepper (adjust to taste)
- Salt and black pepper to taste
- Wooden skewers, soaked in water for 30 minutes to prevent burning

For the Yogurt-Harissa Dip:

- 1 cup Greek yogurt
- 2 tablespoons harissa paste
- 1 tablespoon fresh lemon juice
- 1 clove garlic, minced

- Salt to taste
- Fresh cilantro leaves, for garnish (optional)

Instructions:

For the Moroccan Spiced Chicken Skewers:

1. In a bowl, add the olive oil, ground cumin, ground coriander, smoked paprika, ground cinnamon, ground ginger, ground turmeric, cayenne pepper, salt, and black pepper to create the marinade.

2. Place the chicken cubes in a resealable plastic bag or a shallow dish and pour the marinade over them. Ensure the chicken is well coated. Marinate for at least 15 minutes.

3. Preheat your Air Fryer to 375°F (190°C).

4. Thread the marinated chicken cubes onto the soaked wooden skewers, ensuring evenly distributed.

5. Place the chicken skewers in the Air Fryer basket, ensuring not overcrowded.

6. Cook in the Air Fryer at 375°F (190°C) for approximately 12-15 minutes, turning the skewers halfway through the cooking time. Cook until the chicken is fully cooked and has a nicely browned exterior.

For the Yogurt-Harissa Dip:

1. In a bowl, add the Greek yogurt, harissa paste, fresh lemon juice, minced garlic, and a pinch of salt. Mix sufficiently.

2. Adjust the seasoning to your preference, adding more salt or harissa paste for spiciness.

Assembly:

1. Serve the hot Moroccan Spiced Chicken Skewers with the cool Yogurt-Harissa Dip on the side.

2. Optionally, garnish with fresh cilantro leaves for added flavor.

3. Enjoy your weight-loss-friendly Mediterranean-inspired Moroccan meal!

Nutritional Information (per serving):

- Carbs: 8 grams
- Fats: 9 grams
- Fiber: 2 grams
- Protein: 27 grams

Tuscan-style Turkey and White Bean Soup

Prep Time: 15 minutes
Cook Time: 30 minutes
Number of Servings: 4

Ingredients:

- 1 pound (16 ounces) ground turkey
- 1 tablespoon olive oil
- 1 onion, diced
- 2 carrots, diced
- 2 celery stalks, diced
- 3 cloves garlic, minced
- 1 teaspoon dried oregano
- 1 teaspoon dried basil
- 1/2 teaspoon dried thyme
- 1/2 teaspoon dried rosemary
- 1/4 teaspoon red pepper flakes (adjust to taste)
- 1 can (14 ounces) diced tomatoes, undrained
- 4 cups low-sodium chicken broth
- 2 cans (15 ounces each) white beans, drained and rinsed
- Salt and black pepper to taste
- Fresh parsley, chopped (for garnish)

Instructions:

1. Preheat your Air Fryer to 375°F (190°C).
2. In a large soup pot, heat the olive oil over medium heat. Add the diced onion, carrots, and celery. Sauté for about 5 minutes until the vegetables start to soften.
3. Add the minced garlic, dried oregano, dried basil, dried thyme, dried rosemary, and red pepper flakes to the pot. Cook for an extra 1-2 minutes until the garlic becomes fragrant.
4. Push the sautéed vegetables to one side of the pot and add the ground turkey to the other side. Cook the turkey, breaking it into smaller pieces with a spoon, until it is browned and properly cooked.
5. Stir in the diced tomatoes (with their juices) and the low-sodium chicken broth. Bring the mixture to a simmer.
6. While the soup is simmering, place the drained and rinsed white beans in the Air Fryer basket and cook at 375°F (190°C) for about 10 minutes until heated through and slightly crispy.
7. Add the heated white beans to the simmering soup.
8. Season the soup with salt and black pepper to taste. Adjust the seasoning to your preference.
9. Simmer the soup for an extra 10-15 minutes to allow the flavors to meld together.
10. Serve hot, garnished with chopped fresh parsley.

Nutritional Information (per serving):

- Carbs: 27 grams
- Fats: 10 grams
- Fiber: 7 grams
- Protein: 31 grams

VEGETARIAN AND VEGAN

Eggplant and Zucchini Moussaka

Prep Time: 30 minutes
Cook Time: 30 minutes
Number of Servings: 4

Ingredients:

For the Moussaka:

- 1 large eggplant, sliced into 1/4-inch rounds
- 2 medium zucchinis, sliced into 1/4-inch rounds
- 1 tablespoon olive oil
- 1 onion, finely chopped
- 2 cloves garlic, minced
- 1 pound lean ground turkey
- 1 can (14 ounces) diced tomatoes
- 1 teaspoon dried oregano
- 1 teaspoon dried basil
- Salt and pepper to taste

For the Bechamel Sauce:

- 2 tablespoons olive oil
- 2 tablespoons all-purpose flour
- 1 1/2 cups skim milk
- 1/2 teaspoon nutmeg
- Salt and pepper to taste
- 1/4 cup grated Parmesan cheese

Instructions:

1. Preheat your air fryer to 375°F (190°C).
2. Place the eggplant and zucchini slices in a single layer in the air fryer basket. You may need to work in batches. Air fry for 8-10 minutes or until lightly browned and tender. Set aside.
3. In a large skillet, heat one tablespoon of olive oil over medium heat. Add the chopped onion and minced garlic, sauté until fragrant and translucent.
4. Add the ground turkey to the skillet and cook until it's browned and properly cooked. Break it into small pieces with a spoon as it cooks.
5. Stir in the diced tomatoes, dried oregano, dried basil, salt, and pepper. Let the mixture simmer for about 10 minutes, allowing the flavors to meld. Take it out from heat.
6. In a separate saucepan, heat two tablespoons of olive oil over medium heat. Add the all-purpose flour and cook,

stirring constantly, for 1-2 minutes to make a roux.

7. Gradually whisk in the skim milk until the mixture is smooth and thickened. Add the nutmeg, salt, and pepper, and keep on cooking for another 2-3 minutes, or until the sauce has thickened further.

8. Layer half of the air-fried eggplant and zucchini slices in the bottom of a baking dish. Spread the turkey and tomato mixture evenly over the vegetables.

9. Add the remaining eggplant and zucchini slices on top of the turkey mixture.

10. Pour the bechamel sauce evenly over the top layer of vegetables.

11. Sprinkle the grated Parmesan cheese over the sauce.

12. Bake in a preheated oven at 375°F (190°C) for 25-30 minutes, or until the moussaka is bubbly and the top is golden brown.

Nutritional Information (per serving):

- Carbs: 20g
- Fats: 12g
- Fiber: 6g
- Protein: 28g

Vegan Mediterranean Stuffed Bell Peppers

Prep Time: 25 minutes
Cook Time: 20 minutes
Number of Servings: 4

Ingredients:

- 4 large bell peppers, any color
- 1 cup quinoa
- 2 cups vegetable broth
- 1 can (15 ounces) chickpeas, drained and rinsed
- 1 cup diced tomatoes (canned or fresh)
- 1/2 cup diced cucumber
- 1/4 cup diced red onion
- 1/4 cup chopped fresh parsley
- 2 tablespoons olive oil
- 1 teaspoon dried oregano
- 1/2 teaspoon ground cumin
- Salt and pepper to taste
- Juice of 1 lemon
- 1/4 cup pine nuts, toasted (optional)

Instructions:

1. Preheat your air fryer to 375°F (190°C).

2. Cut the tops off the bell peppers and take out the seeds and membranes. Set aside.

3. In a fine-mesh strainer, rinse the quinoa under cold water until the water runs clear.

4. In a saucepan, add the rinsed quinoa and vegetable broth. Bring to a boil, then reduce the heat to low, cover, and simmer for 15-20 minutes or until the quinoa is cooked and the liquid is absorbed. Take it out from heat and fluff with a fork.

5. In a large bowl, add the cooked quinoa, chickpeas, diced tomatoes, diced cucumber, diced red onion, chopped fresh parsley, olive oil, dried oregano, ground cumin, salt, and pepper. Mix sufficiently to combine all the ingredients.

6. Stuff each bell pepper with the quinoa and vegetable mixture, pressing down gently to pack the filling.

7. Place the stuffed bell peppers in the air fryer basket. You may need to work in batches depending on the size of your air fryer.

8. Air fry the stuffed bell peppers at 375°F (190°C) for 15-20 minutes or until the peppers are tender and slightly charred on the outside.

9. While the peppers are cooking, prepare the lemon drizzle by mixing the lemon juice with a pinch of salt.

10. Once the stuffed bell peppers are done, take them out from the air fryer and drizzle the lemon juice mixture over each pepper.

11. If desired, sprinkle toasted pine nuts over the top for added crunch.

Nutritional Information (per serving):

- Carbs: 56g
- Fats: 11g
- Fiber: 12g
- Protein: 12g

Spinach and Chickpea Curry

Prep Time: 15 minutes
Cook Time: 20 minutes
Number of Servings: 4

Ingredients:

- 1 cup dried chickpeas, soaked overnight and cooked
- 2 tablespoons olive oil
- 1 onion, finely chopped
- 3 cloves garlic, minced
- 1-inch piece of fresh ginger, grated
- 1 teaspoon ground cumin
- 1 teaspoon ground coriander
- 1 teaspoon ground turmeric
- 1 teaspoon paprika
- 1/2 teaspoon ground cinnamon

- 1/4 teaspoon cayenne pepper (adjust to taste)
- 1 can (14 ounces) diced tomatoes
- 1 can (14 ounces) coconut milk
- 1 bunch spinach, washed and chopped
- Salt and pepper to taste
- Juice of 1 lemon
- Fresh cilantro leaves for garnish

Instructions:

1. Preheat your air fryer to 375°F (190°C).
2. In a large skillet, heat the olive oil over medium heat.
3. Add the finely chopped onion and sauté until it becomes translucent, about 3-4 minutes.
4. Add the minced garlic and grated ginger, and sauté for an extra 1-2 minutes until fragrant.
5. Stir in the ground cumin, ground coriander, ground turmeric, paprika, ground cinnamon, and cayenne pepper. Cook for 1-2 minutes to toast the spices.
6. Add the cooked chickpeas to the skillet and stir to coat them with the spice mixture.
7. Pour in the diced tomatoes (with their juice) and coconut milk. Stir to combine, and let the mixture simmer for about 10 minutes, allowing the flavors to meld. If the mixture becomes too thick, you can add a little water to achieve your desired consistency.
8. While the curry is simmering, place the chopped spinach in the air fryer basket and air fry at 375°F (190°C) for 2-3 minutes, or until it wilts and becomes slightly crispy. Set aside.
9. Season the curry with salt and pepper to taste. Squeeze the juice of 1 lemon over the curry and stir to incorporate.
10. To serve, place a portion of the air-fried spinach on each plate and ladle the chickpea curry on top.
11. Garnish with fresh cilantro leaves.

Nutritional Information (per serving):

- Carbs: 38g
- Fats: 19g
- Fiber: 10g
- Protein: 11g

Mediterranean Roasted Vegetable Platter

Prep Time: 15 minutes
Cook Time: 20 minutes
Number of Servings: 4

Ingredients:

- 1 medium eggplant, diced into 1-inch cubes
- 2 medium zucchinis, sliced into rounds
- 1 red bell pepper, sliced into strips
- 1 yellow bell pepper, sliced into strips
- 1 red onion, sliced into wedges
- 2 tablespoons olive oil
- 2 teaspoons dried oregano
- 1 teaspoon dried thyme
- 1 teaspoon dried rosemary
- Salt and pepper to taste
- 1/4 cup chopped fresh parsley
- Juice of 1 lemon
- 1/4 cup crumbled feta cheese (optional)

Instructions:

1. Preheat your air fryer to 375°F (190°C).
2. In a large bowl, add the diced eggplant, sliced zucchinis, red and yellow bell pepper strips, and sliced red onion.
3. Drizzle the olive oil over the vegetables and sprinkle with dried oregano, dried thyme, dried rosemary, salt, and pepper. Toss to coat the vegetables evenly with the seasoning.
4. Place the seasoned vegetables in the air fryer basket in a single layer. You may need to work in batches depending on the size of your air fryer.
5. Air fry the vegetables at 375°F (190°C) for 15-20 minutes, or until tender and have a slight char on the edges. Shake or toss them halfway through the cooking time for even browning.
6. While the vegetables are cooking, chop the fresh parsley and set it aside.
7. Once the vegetables are done, take them out from the air fryer and transfer them to a serving platter.
8. Squeeze the juice of 1 lemon over the roasted vegetables.
9. If desired, sprinkle crumbled feta cheese over the top.
10. Garnish with chopped fresh parsley.

Nutritional Information (per serving, without feta cheese):

- Carbs: 17g
- Fats: 8g
- Fiber: 7g

- Protein: 3g

Cilantro and Lemon Couscous with Dried Fruits and Nuts

Prep Time: 10 minutes
Cook Time: 5 minutes
Number of Servings: 4

Ingredients:

- 1 cup couscous
- 1 1/2 cups boiling water
- 1/2 cup dried apricots, finely diced
- 1/4 cup dried cranberries
- 1/4 cup chopped almonds
- 1/4 cup chopped walnuts
- 1/4 cup fresh cilantro, finely chopped
- Juice and zest of 1 lemon
- 2 tablespoons olive oil
- Salt and pepper to taste

Instructions:

1. Preheat your air fryer to 375°F (190°C).
2. Place the couscous in a heatproof bowl. Pour the boiling water over the couscous, cover with a lid or plastic wrap, and let it sit for 5 minutes. Fluff the couscous with a fork to separate the grains.
3. In a large bowl, add the cooked couscous, finely diced dried apricots, dried cranberries, chopped almonds, chopped walnuts, and finely chopped fresh cilantro.
4. In a separate bowl, whisk the juice and zest of 1 lemon, olive oil, salt, and pepper.
5. Pour the lemon and olive oil dressing over the couscous mixture. Toss everything together until well combined and evenly coated with the dressing.
6. Transfer the couscous mixture to the air fryer basket in an even layer.
7. Air fry the couscous mixture at 375°F (190°C) for 3-4 minutes, or until it is heated through and slightly toasted, stirring or shaking the basket halfway through.
8. Take out the couscous from the air fryer and transfer it to a serving platter.

Nutritional Information (per serving):

- Carbs: 42g
- Fats: 14g
- Fiber: 5g
- Protein: 7g

Vegan Eggplant Parmesan with Spaghetti Squash

Prep Time: 30 minutes
Cook Time: 30 minutes
Number of Servings: 4

Ingredients:

For the Spaghetti Squash:

- 1 medium spaghetti squash, halved and seeds removed
- 1 tablespoon olive oil
- Salt and pepper to taste

For the Vegan Eggplant Parmesan:

- 1 large eggplant, sliced into 1/2-inch rounds
- 1 cup whole wheat breadcrumbs
- 1/4 cup nutritional yeast
- 1 teaspoon dried basil
- 1 teaspoon dried oregano
- 1/2 teaspoon garlic powder
- 1/2 teaspoon onion powder
- 1/2 teaspoon salt
- 1/4 teaspoon black pepper
- 1 cup marinara sauce (store-bought or homemade)
- 1 cup vegan mozzarella cheese, shredded
- Fresh basil leaves for garnish (optional)

Instructions:

1. Preheat your air fryer to 375°F (190°C).
2. Place the halved and seeded spaghetti squash in the air fryer basket, cut side up. Drizzle each half with 1/2 tablespoon of olive oil and season with salt and pepper.
3. Air fry the spaghetti squash at 375°F (190°C) for 20-25 minutes, or until the flesh is tender and easily shreds into spaghetti-like strands with a fork. Take out the strands and set them aside.
4. While the spaghetti squash is cooking, prepare the vegan eggplant parmesan. In a shallow bowl, add the whole wheat breadcrumbs, nutritional yeast, dried basil, dried oregano, garlic powder, onion powder, salt, and black pepper.
5. Dip each eggplant slice into the breadcrumb mixture, ensuring both sides are coated. Place the coated eggplant slices in the air fryer basket in a single layer.
6. Air fry the eggplant slices at 375°F (190°C) for 10-12 minutes, flipping them halfway through, or until golden brown and crispy.
7. In a baking dish, spread a thin layer of marinara sauce. Place the air-fried eggplant slices on top of the sauce. Top each slice with a sprinkle of vegan mozzarella cheese.

8. Bake the assembled eggplant parmesan in the preheated air fryer at 375°F (190°C) for an extra 10-15 minutes, or until the cheese is melted and bubbly.

9. To serve, place a portion of the cooked spaghetti squash on each plate and top it with the vegan eggplant parmesan slices.

10. Garnish with fresh basil leaves if desired.

Nutritional Information (per serving):

- Carbs: 40g
- Fats: 11g
- Fiber: 10g
- Protein: 9g

Spanakopita Stuffed Portobello Mushrooms

Prep Time: 20 minutes
Cook Time: 20 minutes
Number of Servings: 4

Ingredients:

- 4 large Portobello mushrooms, stems removed and cleaned
- 2 cups fresh spinach, chopped
- 1/2 cup crumbled feta cheese
- 1/4 cup diced red onion
- 1/4 cup chopped fresh dill
- 1/4 cup chopped fresh parsley
- 2 cloves garlic, minced
- 2 tablespoons olive oil
- 1/4 teaspoon ground nutmeg
- Salt and pepper to taste
- Cooking spray

Instructions:

1. Preheat your air fryer to 375°F (190°C).

2. In a large skillet, heat one tablespoon of olive oil over medium heat.

3. Add the diced red onion and minced garlic to the skillet. Sauté for 2-3 minutes, or until the onion becomes translucent.

4. Add the chopped spinach to the skillet and cook for another 2-3 minutes, or until the spinach wilts.

5. Take out the skillet from heat and stir in the crumbled feta cheese, chopped fresh dill, chopped fresh parsley, ground nutmeg, salt, and pepper. Set the filling aside.

6. Lightly brush the cleaned Portobello mushroom caps with the remaining one tablespoon of olive oil on both sides.

7. Place the mushroom caps in the air fryer basket, cap side down. Air fry at 375°F (190°C)

for 8-10 minutes, or until the mushrooms begin to soften.

8. Carefully take out the mushroom caps from the air fryer and drain any excess liquid that may have collected inside the caps.

9. Stuff each Portobello mushroom cap with the prepared spinach and feta filling.

10. Return the stuffed mushrooms to the air fryer basket, stuffing side up. Air fry for an extra 8-10 minutes, or until the mushrooms are tender and the filling is heated through and slightly golden on top.

11. Serve the Spanakopita Stuffed Portobello Mushrooms hot and garnish with extra fresh dill and parsley if desired.

Nutritional Information (per serving):

- Carbs: 9g
- Fats: 9g
- Fiber: 3g
- Protein: 7g

Mediterranean Roasted Veggie Tacos with Tahini Sauce

Prep Time: 20 minutes
Cook Time: 20 minutes
Number of Servings: 4

Ingredients:

For the Roasted Veggies:

- 2 cups bell peppers, sliced into strips (use a mix of red, yellow, and green)
- 2 cups zucchini, sliced into rounds
- 1 cup red onion, thinly sliced
- 1 cup cherry tomatoes, halved
- 2 tablespoons olive oil
- 1 teaspoon dried oregano
- 1 teaspoon dried thyme
- Salt and pepper to taste

For the Tahini Sauce:

- 1/2 cup tahini
- Juice of 1 lemon
- 2 cloves garlic, minced
- 2 tablespoons water
- Salt and pepper to taste

For Assembling Tacos:

- 8 small whole wheat tortillas
- 1 cup fresh spinach leaves
- 1/4 cup chopped fresh parsley
- 1/4 cup crumbled feta cheese (optional)

Instructions:

1. Preheat your air fryer to 375°F (190°C).

2. In a large bowl, add the sliced bell peppers, sliced zucchini, thinly sliced red onion, and halved cherry tomatoes.

3. Drizzle the olive oil over the vegetables and sprinkle with dried oregano, dried thyme, salt, and pepper. Toss to coat the vegetables evenly with the seasoning.

4. Place the seasoned vegetables in the air fryer basket in a single layer. You may need to work in batches depending on the size of your air fryer.

5. Air fry the vegetables at 375°F (190°C) for 10-12 minutes, or until tender and slightly charred on the edges, shaking the basket or tossing them halfway through the cooking time.

6. While the veggies are roasting, prepare the tahini sauce. In a small bowl, whisk the tahini, lemon juice, minced garlic, water, salt, and pepper until smooth. If needed, add more water to achieve your desired sauce consistency.

7. Warm the whole wheat tortillas in the air fryer for 1-2 minutes until slightly crispy and warm.

8. To assemble the tacos, spread a spoonful of tahini sauce onto each tortilla.

9. Top each tortilla with a handful of fresh spinach leaves.

10. Add a portion of the roasted veggies on top of the spinach.

11. Sprinkle chopped fresh parsley and crumbled feta cheese (if using) over the veggies.

12. Fold the tortillas in half to create tacos.

13. Serve the Mediterranean Roasted Veggie Tacos with additional tahini sauce on the side for dipping, if desired.

Nutritional Information (per serving, without feta cheese):

- Carbs: 38g
- Fats: 15g
- Fiber: 8g
- Protein: 10g

Vegan Moroccan Lentil Stew

Prep Time: 15 minutes
Cook Time: 30 minutes
Number of Servings: 4

Ingredients:

- 1 cup dried green or brown lentils, rinsed and drained
- 4 cups vegetable broth
- 1 onion, finely chopped
- 2 cloves garlic, minced

- 1 carrot, diced
- 1 red bell pepper, diced
- 1 zucchini, diced
- 1 can (14 ounces) diced tomatoes
- 1 tablespoon olive oil
- 1 tablespoon ground cumin
- 1 teaspoon ground coriander
- 1 teaspoon paprika
- 1/2 teaspoon ground cinnamon
- Salt and pepper to taste
- 1/4 cup chopped fresh cilantro
- Juice of 1 lemon
- Lemon wedges for garnish (optional)

Instructions:

1. Preheat your air fryer to 375°F (190°C).
2. In a large pot, heat the olive oil over medium heat.
3. Add the finely chopped onion and sauté for 2-3 minutes until it becomes translucent.
4. Stir in the minced garlic, ground cumin, ground coriander, paprika, and ground cinnamon. Cook for another 1-2 minutes until the spices are fragrant.
5. Add the diced carrot, red bell pepper, and zucchini to the pot. Sauté for 5-7 minutes, or until the vegetables start to soften.
6. Pour in the rinsed lentils and diced tomatoes (with their juice). Stir to combine.
7. Add the vegetable broth, salt, and pepper. Bring the mixture to a boil, then reduce the heat to low, cover, and let it simmer for 20-25 minutes, or until the lentils are tender and the stew has thickened.
8. While the stew is simmering, place the lemon wedges in the air fryer basket and air fry at 375°F (190°C) for 3-4 minutes until slightly caramelized. Set them aside for garnish.
9. Once the lentil stew is done, remove it from heat and stir in the chopped fresh cilantro and the juice of 1 lemon.
10. Serve the Vegan Moroccan Lentil Stew hot, garnished with the air-fried lemon wedges, if desired.

Nutritional Information (per serving):

- Carbs: 45g
- Fats: 4g
- Fiber: 14g
- Protein: 15g

Artichoke and Sun-Dried Tomato Stuffed Peppers

Prep Time: 20 minutes
Cook Time: 20 minutes
Number of Servings: 4

Ingredients:

- 4 large bell peppers, any color
- 1 cup cooked quinoa
- 1 can (14 ounces) artichoke hearts, drained and chopped
- 1/2 cup sun-dried tomatoes, chopped
- 1/4 cup Kalamata olives, pitted and chopped
- 1/4 cup fresh basil leaves, chopped
- 2 cloves garlic, minced
- 2 tablespoons olive oil
- Salt and pepper to taste
- 1/4 cup crumbled feta cheese (optional)
- Fresh basil leaves for garnish

Instructions:

1. Preheat your air fryer to 375°F (190°C).
2. Cut the tops off the bell peppers and take out the seeds and membranes. Set aside.
3. In a large bowl, add the cooked quinoa, chopped artichoke hearts, chopped sun-dried tomatoes, chopped Kalamata olives, chopped fresh basil leaves, minced garlic, olive oil, salt, and pepper. Mix sufficiently to combine all the ingredients.
4. Stuff each bell pepper with the quinoa and vegetable mixture, pressing down gently to pack the filling.
5. Place the stuffed bell peppers in the air fryer basket. You may need to work in batches depending on the size of your air fryer.
6. Air fry the stuffed bell peppers at 375°F (190°C) for 15-20 minutes, or until the peppers are tender and the filling is heated through.
7. If desired, sprinkle crumbled feta cheese over the top of each stuffed pepper during the last 5 minutes of cooking for added flavor.
8. Garnish the Artichoke and Sun-Dried Tomato Stuffed Peppers with fresh basil leaves.

Nutritional Information (per serving, without feta cheese):

- Carbs: 33g
- Fats: 9g
- Fiber: 7g
- Protein: 6g

Mediterranean Stuffed Bell Peppers with Quinoa and Chickpeas

Prep Time: 25 minutes
Cook Time: 20 minutes
Number of Servings: 4

Ingredients:

- 4 large bell peppers, any color
- 1 cup quinoa
- 2 cups vegetable broth
- 1 can (15 ounces) chickpeas, drained and rinsed
- 1 cup diced tomatoes (canned or fresh)
- 1/2 cup diced cucumber
- 1/4 cup diced red onion
- 1/4 cup chopped fresh parsley
- 2 tablespoons olive oil
- 1 teaspoon dried oregano
- 1/2 teaspoon ground cumin
- Salt and pepper to taste
- Juice of 1 lemon
- 1/4 cup pine nuts, toasted (optional)

Instructions:

1. Preheat your air fryer to 375°F (190°C).
2. Cut the tops off the bell peppers and take out the seeds and membranes. Set aside.
3. In a fine-mesh strainer, rinse the quinoa under cold water until the water runs clear.
4. In a saucepan, add the rinsed quinoa and vegetable broth. Bring to a boil, then reduce the heat to low, cover, and simmer for 15-20 minutes or until the quinoa is cooked and the liquid is absorbed. Take it out from heat and fluff with a fork.
5. In a large bowl, add the cooked quinoa, chickpeas, diced tomatoes, diced cucumber, diced red onion, chopped fresh parsley, olive oil, dried oregano, ground cumin, salt, and pepper. Mix sufficiently to combine all the ingredients.
6. Stuff each bell pepper with the quinoa and vegetable mixture, pressing down gently to pack the filling.
7. Place the stuffed bell peppers in the air fryer basket. You may need to work in batches depending on the size of your air fryer.
8. Air fry the stuffed bell peppers at 375°F (190°C) for 15-20 minutes or until the peppers are tender and slightly charred on the outside.
9. While the peppers are cooking, prepare the lemon drizzle by mixing the lemon juice with a pinch of salt.

10. Once the stuffed bell peppers are done, take them out from the air fryer and drizzle the lemon juice mixture over each pepper.

11. If desired, sprinkle toasted pine nuts over the top for added crunch.

Nutritional Information (per serving):

- Carbs: 56g
- Fats: 11g
- Fiber: 12g
- Protein: 12g

Vegan Greek Spinach and Rice Stuffed Tomatoes

Prep Time: 30 minutes
Cook Time: 25 minutes
Number of Servings: 4

Ingredients:

- 4 large tomatoes
- 1 cup long-grain white rice
- 2 cups vegetable broth
- 2 tablespoons olive oil
- 1 onion, finely chopped
- 2 cloves garlic, minced
- 4 cups fresh spinach, chopped
- 1/4 cup fresh dill, chopped
- 1/4 cup fresh parsley, chopped
- 1/4 cup fresh mint leaves, chopped
- 1/4 cup pine nuts
- Salt and pepper to taste
- Juice of 1 lemon

Instructions:

1. Preheat your air fryer to 375°F (190°C).

2. Cut the tops off the tomatoes and carefully scoop out the pulp and seeds. Reserve the pulp in a separate bowl.

3. Sprinkle the insides of the hollowed-out tomatoes with a pinch of salt and place them in the air fryer basket.

4. Air fry the tomatoes at 375°F (190°C) for 5-7 minutes or until they begin to soften. Take them out from the air fryer and set aside.

5. In a fine-mesh strainer, rinse the rice under cold water until the water runs clear.

6. In a saucepan, add the rinsed rice and vegetable broth. Bring to a boil, then reduce the heat to low, cover, and simmer for 15 minutes or until the rice is cooked and the liquid is absorbed. Take it out from heat and let it cool slightly.

7. In a large skillet, heat the olive oil over medium heat.

8. Add the finely chopped onion and sauté for 2-3

minutes until it becomes translucent.

9. Stir in the minced garlic and sauté for an extra minute until fragrant.

10. Add the chopped spinach and reserved tomato pulp to the skillet. Cook for 3-4 minutes, or until the spinach wilts and the tomato pulp breaks down.

11. In a large mixing bowl, add the cooked rice, sautéed spinach and tomato mixture, chopped fresh dill, chopped fresh parsley, chopped fresh mint leaves, pine nuts, salt, and pepper. Mix sufficiently to combine all the ingredients.

12. Carefully stuff each air-fried tomato with the rice and spinach mixture, pressing down gently to pack the filling.

13. Place the stuffed tomatoes back in the air fryer basket.

14. Air fry the stuffed tomatoes at 375°F (190°C) for an extra 10-12 minutes, or until the tomatoes are tender and slightly caramelized.

15. Drizzle the juice of 1 lemon over the stuffed tomatoes before serving.

Nutritional Information (per serving):

- Carbs: 59g
- Fats: 11g
- Fiber: 7g
- Protein: 6g

Moroccan Chickpea and Vegetable Tagine

Prep Time: 20 minutes
Cook Time: 25 minutes
Number of Servings: 4

Ingredients:

- 1 tablespoon olive oil
- 1 onion, finely chopped
- 2 cloves garlic, minced
- 1 teaspoon ground cumin
- 1 teaspoon ground coriander
- 1/2 teaspoon ground cinnamon
- 1/2 teaspoon ground paprika
- 1/4 teaspoon ground turmeric
- 1/4 teaspoon ground ginger
- 1/4 teaspoon cayenne pepper (adjust to taste)
- 2 carrots, peeled and diced
- 1 zucchini, diced
- 1 red bell pepper, diced
- 1 can (14 ounces) diced tomatoes
- 1 can (14 ounces) chickpeas, drained and rinsed
- 1 cup vegetable broth

- Salt and pepper to taste
- 1/4 cup chopped fresh cilantro
- Juice of 1 lemon
- Lemon wedges for garnish (optional)

Instructions:

1. Preheat your air fryer to 375°F (190°C).
2. In a large skillet, heat the olive oil over medium heat.
3. Add the finely chopped onion and sauté for 2-3 minutes until it becomes translucent.
4. Stir in the minced garlic and sauté for an extra minute until fragrant.
5. Add the ground cumin, ground coriander, ground cinnamon, ground paprika, ground turmeric, ground ginger, and cayenne pepper (adjust to taste) to the skillet. Cook for 1-2 minutes until the spices are fragrant.
6. Add the diced carrots, diced zucchini, and diced red bell pepper to the skillet. Sauté for 5-7 minutes, or until the vegetables start to soften.
7. Stir in the diced tomatoes, chickpeas, and vegetable broth. Season with salt and pepper to taste.
8. Transfer the mixture to the air fryer basket.
9. Air fry the tagine mixture at 375°F (190°C) for 15-20 minutes, or until the vegetables are tender and the flavors are well combined, stirring occasionally.
10. While the tagine is cooking, prepare the cilantro and lemon garnish by mixing the chopped cilantro with the juice of 1 lemon.
11. Once the tagine is done, remove it from the air fryer and drizzle the cilantro and lemon mixture over the top.
12. Serve the Moroccan Chickpea and Vegetable Tagine hot, garnished with lemon wedges if desired.

Nutritional Information (per serving):

- Carbs: 42g
- Fats: 5g
- Fiber: 11g
- Protein: 10g

Eggplant and Lentil Moussaka

Prep Time: 30 minutes
Cook Time: 40 minutes
Number of Servings: 6

Ingredients:

For the Eggplant Layer:

- 2 large eggplants, sliced into 1/2-inch rounds

- 2 tablespoons olive oil
- Salt and pepper to taste

For the Lentil Filling:
- 1 cup green or brown lentils, rinsed and drained
- 3 cups vegetable broth
- 1 onion, finely chopped
- 3 cloves garlic, minced
- 1 can (14 ounces) diced tomatoes
- 2 teaspoons dried oregano
- 1 teaspoon ground cinnamon
- Salt and pepper to taste

For the Bechamel Sauce:
- 2 tablespoons olive oil
- 2 tablespoons all-purpose flour
- 2 cups unsweetened almond milk (or any plant-based milk)
- 1/4 teaspoon ground nutmeg
- Salt and pepper to taste

Instructions:
1. Preheat your air fryer to 375°F (190°C).
2. Place the eggplant slices in a single layer in the air fryer basket. You may need to work in batches depending on the size of your air fryer.
3. Air fry the eggplant slices at 375°F (190°C) for 10-12 minutes, flipping them halfway through, or until tender and slightly browned. Remove and set aside.
4. In a saucepan, add the rinsed lentils and vegetable broth. Bring to a boil, then reduce the heat to low, cover, and simmer for 20-25 minutes, or until the lentils are tender and the liquid is absorbed. Take it out from heat and set aside.
5. In a large skillet, heat two tablespoons of olive oil over medium heat.
6. Add the finely chopped onion and sauté for 2-3 minutes until it becomes translucent.
7. Stir in the minced garlic and sauté for an extra minute until fragrant.
8. Add the diced tomatoes, dried oregano, ground cinnamon, salt, and pepper to the skillet. Cook for 5-7 minutes, or until the mixture thickens.
9. Add the cooked lentils to the tomato mixture and stir to combine. Take it out from heat.
10. To make the bechamel sauce, in a separate saucepan, heat two tablespoons of olive oil over medium heat.
11. Stir in the all-purpose flour and cook for 1-2 minutes to form a roux.

12. Gradually whisk in the unsweetened almond milk until the mixture thickens and becomes smooth.

13. Season the bechamel sauce with ground nutmeg, salt, and pepper to taste.

14. To assemble the moussaka, in a baking dish, layer half of the air-fried eggplant slices on the bottom.

15. Spread the lentil and tomato mixture over the eggplant layer.

16. Top the lentil mixture with the remaining eggplant slices.

17. Pour the bechamel sauce evenly over the top layer of eggplant.

18. Air fry the assembled moussaka at 375°F (190°C) for 15-20 minutes, or until it is heated through and the top is golden brown.

19. Remove from the air fryer and let it cool slightly before serving.

Nutritional Information (per serving):

- Carbs: 40g
- Fats: 8g
- Fiber: 13g
- Protein: 12g

Vegan Italian Artichoke and Spinach Lasagna

Prep Time: 30 minutes
Cook Time: 25 minutes
Number of Servings: 6

Ingredients:

For the Lasagna:

- 9 lasagna noodles (whole wheat if available)
- 1 can (14 ounces) artichoke hearts, drained and chopped
- 2 cups fresh spinach, chopped
- 1/2 cup sun-dried tomatoes, chopped
- 1/2 cup roasted red bell peppers, chopped
- 1 cup firm tofu, crumbled
- 1/2 cup nutritional yeast
- 1/2 teaspoon garlic powder
- Salt and pepper to taste

For the Tomato Sauce:

- 1 can (14 ounces) diced tomatoes
- 1/2 cup tomato sauce
- 2 cloves garlic, minced
- 1 teaspoon dried basil
- 1 teaspoon dried oregano
- Salt and pepper to taste

For the Bechamel Sauce:

- 2 tablespoons olive oil

- 2 tablespoons all-purpose flour
- 2 cups unsweetened almond milk (or any plant-based milk)
- 1/4 teaspoon ground nutmeg
- Salt and pepper to taste

Instructions:

1. Preheat your air fryer to 375°F (190°C).
2. Cook the lasagna noodles according to the package instructions until al dente. Drain, rinse with cold water, and set aside.
3. In a mixing bowl, add the chopped artichoke hearts, chopped fresh spinach, chopped sun-dried tomatoes, chopped roasted red bell peppers, crumbled firm tofu, nutritional yeast, garlic powder, salt, and pepper. Mix sufficiently to create the filling.
4. To make the tomato sauce, in a saucepan, add the diced tomatoes, tomato sauce, minced garlic, dried basil, dried oregano, salt, and pepper. Simmer over low heat for 10-15 minutes until the sauce thickens. Take it out from heat and set aside.
5. To make the bechamel sauce, in a separate saucepan, heat two tablespoons of olive oil over medium heat.
6. Stir in the all-purpose flour and cook for 1-2 minutes to form a roux.
7. Gradually whisk in the unsweetened almond milk until the mixture thickens and becomes smooth.
8. Season the bechamel sauce with ground nutmeg, salt, and pepper to taste.
9. In a baking dish that fits your air fryer basket, start assembling the lasagna layers. Begin with a layer of lasagna noodles, followed by a layer of the vegetable and tofu filling, a layer of tomato sauce, and a drizzle of bechamel sauce.
10. Repeat the layers until all the ingredients are used up, finishing with a layer of bechamel sauce on top.
11. Place the assembled lasagna in the air fryer basket.
12. Air fry the lasagna at 375°F (190°C) for 15-20 minutes, or until it is heated through and the top is golden brown.
13. Take out the lasagna from the air fryer and let it cool slightly before serving.

Nutritional Information (per serving):

- Carbs: 39g
- Fats: 11g
- Fiber: 6g

- Protein: 12g

Italian Eggplant and Zucchini Ratatouille

Prep Time: 20 minutes
Cook Time: 25 minutes
Number of Servings: 4

Ingredients:

- 1 large eggplant, diced
- 2 medium zucchinis, diced
- 1 red bell pepper, diced
- 1 yellow bell pepper, diced
- 1 onion, finely chopped
- 3 cloves garlic, minced
- 1 can (14 ounces) diced tomatoes
- 2 tablespoons olive oil
- 1 teaspoon dried basil
- 1 teaspoon dried oregano
- 1/2 teaspoon dried thyme
- Salt and pepper to taste
- Fresh basil leaves for garnish (optional)

Instructions:

1. Preheat your air fryer to 375°F (190°C).
2. In a large mixing bowl, add the diced eggplant, diced zucchinis, diced red bell pepper, diced yellow bell pepper, finely chopped onion, and minced garlic.
3. Drizzle two tablespoons of olive oil over the vegetables and toss to coat them evenly.
4. Transfer the coated vegetables to the air fryer basket.
5. Air fry the vegetables at 375°F (190°C) for 15-20 minutes, shaking the basket or stirring the vegetables halfway through, until tender and slightly caramelized.
6. In a saucepan, add the can of diced tomatoes (with their juice), dried basil, dried oregano, dried thyme, salt, and pepper. Simmer over low heat for 5-7 minutes to create the tomato sauce.
7. Once the vegetables are done air frying, transfer them to a serving dish.
8. Pour the tomato sauce over the air-fried vegetables and gently stir to combine.
9. Garnish with fresh basil leaves if desired.

Nutritional Information (per serving):

- Carbs: 18g
- Fats: 7g
- Fiber: 6g
- Protein: 2g

Greek Vegan Spanakopita with Tofu and Spinach

Prep Time: 30 minutes
Cook Time: 25 minutes
Number of Servings: 4

Ingredients:

For the Filling:

- 1 block (14 ounces) firm tofu, crumbled
- 6 cups fresh spinach, chopped
- 1 onion, finely chopped
- 3 cloves garlic, minced
- 1/4 cup fresh dill, chopped
- 1/4 cup fresh parsley, chopped
- 1/4 cup nutritional yeast
- Salt and pepper to taste
- Olive oil for sautéing

For the Phyllo Pastry:

- 8 sheets of phyllo pastry
- Olive oil for brushing

Instructions:

1. Preheat your air fryer to 375°F (190°C).
2. In a large skillet, heat a bit of olive oil over medium heat.
3. Add the finely chopped onion and sauté for 2-3 minutes until it becomes translucent.
4. Stir in the minced garlic and sauté for an extra minute until fragrant.
5. Add the chopped spinach to the skillet and sauté until it wilts and most of the liquid evaporates. Take it out from heat and set aside.
6. In a mixing bowl, add the crumbled firm tofu, chopped fresh dill, chopped fresh parsley, nutritional yeast, sautéed spinach mixture, salt, and pepper. Mix sufficiently to create the filling.
7. Lay out one sheet of phyllo pastry and brush it lightly with olive oil. Place another sheet on top and brush it with oil as well. Repeat until you have four sheets stacked on top of each other.
8. Spread half of the tofu and spinach filling evenly over the layered phyllo pastry.
9. Continue layering the remaining four sheets of phyllo pastry on top, brushing each sheet with olive oil.
10. Spread the remaining filling over the top layer of phyllo pastry.
11. Fold in the edges of the phyllo pastry to encase the filling.

12. Place the assembled spanakopita in the air fryer basket.

13. Air fry the spanakopita at 375°F (190°C) for 15-20 minutes, or until the phyllo pastry is crispy and golden brown.

14. Take out the spanakopita from the air fryer and let it cool slightly before serving.

Nutritional Information (per serving):

- Carbs: 23g
- Fats: 14g
- Fiber: 4g
- Protein: 15g

Moroccan Chickpea and Eggplant Tagine

Prep Time: 20 minutes
Cook Time: 25 minutes
Number of Servings: 4

Ingredients:

- 1 large eggplant, diced
- 1 can (14 ounces) chickpeas, drained and rinsed
- 1 onion, finely chopped
- 2 cloves garlic, minced
- 1 can (14 ounces) diced tomatoes
- 1/2 cup vegetable broth
- 1/4 cup dried apricots, chopped
- 1/4 cup sliced almonds
- 2 tablespoons olive oil
- 2 teaspoons ground cumin
- 1 teaspoon ground coriander
- 1/2 teaspoon ground cinnamon
- 1/4 teaspoon ground turmeric
- 1/4 teaspoon cayenne pepper (adjust to taste)
- Salt and pepper to taste
- Fresh cilantro leaves for garnish (optional)

Instructions:

1. Preheat your air fryer to 375°F (190°C).

2. Place the diced eggplant in the air fryer basket.

3. Air fry the eggplant at 375°F (190°C) for 10-12 minutes, or until it is tender and slightly browned. Remove and set aside.

4. In a large skillet, heat two tablespoons of olive oil over medium heat.

5. Add the finely chopped onion and sauté for 2-3 minutes until it becomes translucent.

6. Stir in the minced garlic and sauté for an extra minute until fragrant.

7. Add the ground cumin, ground coriander, ground cinnamon, ground turmeric, and cayenne pepper (adjust to taste) to the skillet. Cook for 1-2 minutes until the spices are fragrant.

8. Stir in the diced tomatoes, vegetable broth, and chopped dried apricots. Simmer for 5-7 minutes until the mixture thickens.

9. Add the air-fried eggplant, drained and rinsed chickpeas, and sliced almonds to the skillet. Season with salt and pepper to taste.

10. Continue to simmer for an extra 5 minutes, allowing all the flavors to meld together.

11. Garnish the tagine with fresh cilantro leaves if desired.

Nutritional Information (per serving):

- Carbs: 35g
- Fats: 10g
- Fiber: 10g
- Protein: 10g

Mediterranean Stuffed Acorn Squash with Bulgur

Prep Time: 20 minutes
Cook Time: 25 minutes
Number of Servings: 4

Ingredients:

- 2 acorn squashes, halved and seeds removed
- 1 cup bulgur wheat
- 2 cups vegetable broth
- 1 onion, finely chopped
- 2 cloves garlic, minced
- 1 red bell pepper, diced
- 1 yellow bell pepper, diced
- 1 zucchini, diced
- 1/2 cup cherry tomatoes, halved
- 1/4 cup Kalamata olives, pitted and sliced
- 2 tablespoons olive oil
- 1 teaspoon dried oregano
- 1/2 teaspoon dried basil
- Salt and pepper to taste
- Fresh parsley leaves for garnish (optional)

Instructions:

1. Preheat your air fryer to 375°F (190°C).

2. Place the halved acorn squashes in the air fryer basket, cut side down.

3. Air fry the acorn squashes at 375°F (190°C) for 12-15 minutes, or until slightly tender. Remove and set aside.

4. In a saucepan, add the bulgur wheat and vegetable broth. Bring to a boil, then reduce

the heat to low, cover, and simmer for 12-15 minutes, or until the bulgur is tender and the liquid is absorbed. Take it out from heat and set aside.

5. In a large skillet, heat two tablespoons of olive oil over medium heat.

6. Add the finely chopped onion and sauté for 2-3 minutes until it becomes translucent.

7. Stir in the minced garlic and sauté for an extra minute until fragrant.

8. Add the diced red bell pepper, diced yellow bell pepper, and diced zucchini to the skillet. Sauté for 5-7 minutes, or until the vegetables are tender.

9. Stir in the halved cherry tomatoes, sliced Kalamata olives, dried oregano, dried basil, salt, and pepper. Cook for an extra 2-3 minutes until the tomatoes are slightly softened.

10. Fluff the cooked bulgur with a fork and add it to the skillet with the sautéed vegetables. Mix sufficiently to combine all the ingredients.

11. Carefully stuff each acorn squash half with the bulgur and vegetable mixture.

12. Place the stuffed acorn squashes back in the air fryer basket.

13. Air fry the stuffed acorn squashes at 375°F (190°C) for 10-12 minutes, or until heated through and the tops are lightly browned.

14. Garnish with fresh parsley leaves if desired.

Nutritional Information (per serving):

- Carbs: 45g
- Fats: 10g
- Fiber: 10g
- Protein: 7g

Vegan Italian Pasta Primavera with Lemon Garlic Sauce

Prep Time: 15 minutes
Cook Time: 15 minutes
Number of Servings: 4

Ingredients:

For the Pasta:

- 8 ounces whole wheat pasta (penne or spaghetti)
- 2 cups broccoli florets
- 1 cup cherry tomatoes, halved
- 1 cup bell peppers (red, yellow, or green), thinly sliced
- 1 cup zucchini, thinly sliced
- 1/2 cup carrots, thinly sliced
- 2 tablespoons olive oil

- Salt and pepper to taste

For the Lemon Garlic Sauce:

- Juice of 2 lemons
- 3 cloves garlic, minced
- 2 tablespoons olive oil
- Zest of 1 lemon
- 1/4 cup fresh basil, chopped
- Salt and pepper to taste
- Red pepper flakes (optional)

Instructions:

1. Preheat your air fryer to 375°F (190°C).
2. In a large pot, cook the whole wheat pasta according to the package instructions until al dente. Drain and set aside.
3. While the pasta is cooking, place the broccoli florets, halved cherry tomatoes, thinly sliced bell peppers, thinly sliced zucchini, and thinly sliced carrots in the air fryer basket.
4. Drizzle two tablespoons of olive oil over the vegetables and season with salt and pepper to taste.
5. Air fry the vegetables at 375°F (190°C) for 8-10 minutes, shaking the basket or stirring the vegetables halfway through, until tender and slightly caramelized. Remove and set aside.
6. In a small bowl, whisk the lemon juice, minced garlic, two tablespoons of olive oil, lemon zest, chopped fresh basil, salt, and pepper. Add red pepper flakes for a bit of heat if desired.
7. In a large mixing bowl, add the cooked pasta and air-fried vegetables.
8. Pour the lemon garlic sauce over the pasta and vegetables, tossing to coat everything evenly.
9. Serve your Vegan Italian Pasta Primavera with Lemon Garlic Sauce hot, garnished with additional fresh basil if desired.

Nutritional Information (per serving):

- Carbs: 54g
- Fats: 15g
- Fiber: 11g
- Protein: 10g

PASTA AND GRAINS

Greek Spinach and Feta Stuffed Shells

Prep Time: 20 minutes
Cook Time: 25 minutes
Number of Servings: 4

Ingredients:

For the Stuffed Shells:

- 20 jumbo pasta shells
- 2 cups fresh spinach, chopped
- 1 cup crumbled feta cheese
- 1/2 cup low-fat ricotta cheese
- 1/4 cup grated Parmesan cheese
- 1/4 cup finely chopped red onion
- 2 cloves garlic, minced
- 1/2 teaspoon dried oregano
- 1/2 teaspoon dried basil
- Salt and pepper to taste

For the Tomato Sauce:

- 1 can (14 ounces) diced tomatoes
- 1/2 cup tomato sauce
- 2 cloves garlic, minced
- 1/2 teaspoon dried oregano
- 1/2 teaspoon dried basil
- Salt and pepper to taste

For the Topping:

- 1/4 cup grated Parmesan cheese
- Fresh basil leaves, for garnish

Instructions:

1. **Prepare the Stuffed Shells:**

   - Cook the jumbo pasta shells according to package instructions until al dente. Drain and set aside.
   - In a mixing bowl, add chopped fresh spinach, crumbled feta cheese, low-fat ricotta cheese, grated Parmesan cheese, finely chopped red onion, minced garlic, dried oregano, dried basil, salt, and pepper. Mix sufficiently.

2. **Stuff the Shells:**

   - Preheat your air fryer to 350°F (175°C).
   - Carefully stuff each cooked pasta shell with the spinach and feta mixture, ensuring well-filled but not overflowing.

3. **Prepare the Tomato Sauce:**

- In a separate bowl, add the diced tomatoes, tomato sauce, minced garlic, dried oregano, dried basil, salt, and pepper.

4. **Air Fry the Stuffed Shells:**
   - Place the stuffed shells in the air fryer basket in a single layer.
   - Air fry at 350°F (175°C) for 10-12 minutes or until the shells are heated through and slightly crispy on the outside.

5. **Serve:**
   - Pour the tomato sauce over the air-fried stuffed shells.
   - Sprinkle with grated Parmesan cheese.

6. **Garnish:**
   - Garnish with fresh basil leaves.

Nutritional Information (per serving):

- Carbs: 44g
- Fats: 15g
- Fiber: 5g
- Protein: 18g

Lebanese Lentil and Rice Pilaf

Prep Time: 15 minutes
Cook Time: 25 minutes
Number of Servings: 4

Ingredients:

- 1 cup brown or green lentils, rinsed and drained
- 1 cup long-grain brown rice
- 2 tablespoons olive oil
- 1 onion, finely chopped
- 2 cloves garlic, minced
- 1 teaspoon ground cumin
- 1/2 teaspoon ground coriander
- 1/2 teaspoon ground turmeric
- 1/4 teaspoon ground cinnamon
- 1/4 teaspoon cayenne pepper (adjust to taste)
- 4 cups low-sodium vegetable broth
- Salt and black pepper to taste
- Fresh cilantro or parsley leaves, for garnish
- Lemon wedges, for serving

Instructions:

1. **Prepare Lentils and Rice:**
   - Rinse the lentils and rice separately under cold water and set them aside.

2. **Sauté Onions and Garlic:**

- In a large skillet or frying pan, heat the olive oil over medium heat.
- Add the finely chopped onion and cook until it becomes translucent, about 3-4 minutes.
- Stir in the minced garlic and cook for an extra 30 seconds until fragrant.

3. **Add Spices:**
   - Add ground cumin, ground coriander, ground turmeric, ground cinnamon, and cayenne pepper to the onion and garlic mixture. Stir sufficiently to combine and cook for another minute to toast the spices.

4. **Combine Lentils and Rice:**
   - Add the rinsed lentils and rice to the skillet, stirring to coat them with the onion and spice mixture.

5. **Air Fry the Mixture:**
   - Preheat your air fryer to 350°F (175°C).
   - Transfer the lentil and rice mixture to the air fryer basket.
   - Air fry for about 5 minutes to slightly toast the lentils and rice, stirring occasionally.

6. **Add Broth:**
   - Pour in the low-sodium vegetable broth into the air fryer basket, covering the lentils and rice mixture. Season with salt and black pepper to taste.

7. **Air Fry the Pilaf:**
   - Continue air frying at 350°F (175°C) for 15-20 minutes or until the lentils and rice are tender and the liquid is absorbed. Stir occasionally during cooking.

8. **Serve:**
   - Once cooked, transfer the Lebanese Lentil and Rice Pilaf to a serving dish.
   - Garnish with fresh cilantro or parsley leaves and serve with lemon wedges for squeezing over the pilaf.

Nutritional Information (per serving):
- Carbs: 62g
- Fats: 7g

- Fiber: 11g
- Protein: 16g

Mediterranean Farro Risotto with Roasted Tomatoes

Prep Time: 10 minutes
Cook Time: 25 minutes
Number of Servings: 4

Ingredients:

For the Roasted Tomatoes:

- 2 cups cherry tomatoes
- 1 tablespoon olive oil
- Salt and black pepper to taste

For the Farro Risotto:

- 1 cup pearled farro
- 1 small onion, finely chopped
- 2 cloves garlic, minced
- 1 tablespoon olive oil
- 3 cups low-sodium vegetable broth
- 1/2 cup dry white wine (optional)
- 1/2 cup grated Parmesan cheese
- 1/4 cup fresh basil leaves, chopped
- Salt and black pepper to taste

Instructions:

1. **Roast the Tomatoes:**
   - Preheat your air fryer to 375°F (190°C).
   - In a bowl, toss the cherry tomatoes with olive oil, salt, and black pepper.
   - Place the seasoned tomatoes in the air fryer basket and roast for 10-12 minutes or until blistered and slightly caramelized. Set aside.

2. **Prepare the Farro:**
   - Rinse the pearled farro under cold water and drain.
   - In a large skillet or frying pan, heat one tablespoon of olive oil over medium heat.
   - Add the finely chopped onion and cook until it becomes translucent, about 3-4 minutes.
   - Stir in the minced garlic and cook for an extra 30 seconds until fragrant.
   - Add the drained farro to the skillet, stirring to coat it with the onion and garlic mixture.

3. **Add Liquid and Cook:**
   - If using, pour in the dry white wine and

stir until it's mostly absorbed by the farro.

- Gradually add the low-sodium vegetable broth, one ladle at a time, stirring frequently. Wait until each addition is mostly absorbed before adding more. Continue until the farro is tender and creamy, about 20-25 minutes.

4. **Finish the Risotto:**
   - Stir in the grated Parmesan cheese and chopped fresh basil.
   - Season with salt and black pepper to taste.

5. **Serve:**
   - Divide the Mediterranean Farro Risotto into serving bowls.
   - Top each portion with the roasted tomatoes.

Nutritional Information (per serving):

- Carbs: 56g
- Fats: 9g
- Fiber: 8g
- Protein: 12g

Saffron-infused Moroccan Couscous

Prep Time: 15 minutes
Cook Time: 20 minutes
Number of Servings: 4

Ingredients:

- 1 cup whole wheat couscous
- 2 cups low-sodium vegetable broth
- 1/4 teaspoon saffron threads
- 1 tablespoon olive oil
- 1 small onion, finely chopped
- 2 cloves garlic, minced
- 1 teaspoon ground cumin
- 1/2 teaspoon ground coriander
- 1/2 teaspoon ground paprika
- 1/4 teaspoon ground cinnamon
- Salt and black pepper to taste
- 1/4 cup slivered almonds, toasted
- 1/4 cup fresh cilantro leaves, chopped
- Lemon wedges, for serving

Instructions:

1. **Infuse Saffron:**
   - In a small bowl, add the saffron threads with one tablespoon of hot water. Allow them to steep and

infuse for a few minutes.

2. **Prepare Couscous:**
   - Place the whole wheat couscous in a large mixing bowl.
   - In a saucepan, heat the low-sodium vegetable broth until it simmers. Pour the hot broth over the couscous, covering it completely.
   - Cover the bowl with a lid or plastic wrap and let it sit for about 5 minutes until the couscous absorbs the broth.

3. **Sauté Onion and Spices:**
   - In a large skillet or frying pan, heat the olive oil over medium heat.
   - Add the finely chopped onion and cook until it becomes translucent, about 3-4 minutes.
   - Stir in the minced garlic, ground cumin, ground coriander, ground paprika, ground cinnamon, salt, and black pepper. Cook for another 1-2 minutes until fragrant.

4. **Combine Couscous and Saffron:**
   - Fluff the prepared couscous with a fork to separate the grains.
   - Pour the saffron infusion over the couscous and gently toss to distribute the saffron evenly.

5. **Mix and Toast:**
   - Add the sautéed onion and spice mixture to the couscous. Mix sufficiently to combine.
   - Toast the slivered almonds in the air fryer at 350°F (175°C) for 2-3 minutes until lightly browned.

6. **Serve:**
   - Serve the Saffron-infused Moroccan Couscous garnished with toasted slivered almonds, fresh cilantro leaves, and lemon wedges for squeezing over the couscous.

Nutritional Information (per serving):

- Carbs: 43g
- Fats: 7g
- Fiber: 6g
- Protein: 7g

Lemon Garlic Shrimp and Asparagus Orzo

Prep Time: 15 minutes
Cook Time: 20 minutes
Number of Servings: 4

Ingredients:

- 1 cup whole wheat orzo pasta
- 1 pound large shrimp, peeled and deveined
- 1 bunch fresh asparagus, trimmed and cut into bite-sized pieces
- 2 tablespoons olive oil
- 4 cloves garlic, minced
- Zest of 1 lemon
- Juice of 1 lemon
- 1/2 teaspoon dried oregano
- Salt and black pepper to taste
- Fresh parsley leaves, for garnish
- Lemon wedges, for serving

Instructions:

1. **Prepare Orzo:**
   - Cook the whole wheat orzo pasta according to package instructions until al dente. Drain and set aside.
2. **Season Shrimp and Asparagus:**
   - In a large mixing bowl, add the peeled and deveined shrimp with the trimmed and cut asparagus pieces.
   - Drizzle with one tablespoon of olive oil, minced garlic, lemon zest, dried oregano, salt, and black pepper. Toss to coat the shrimp and asparagus evenly.
3. **Air Fry Shrimp and Asparagus:**
   - Preheat your air fryer to 375°F (190°C).
   - Place the seasoned shrimp and asparagus in the air fryer basket in a single layer.
   - Air fry for about 5-7 minutes or until the shrimp are pink and opaque and the asparagus is tender, shaking the basket halfway through.
4. **Sauté Cooked Orzo:**
   - In a large skillet or frying pan, heat the remaining one tablespoon of olive oil over medium heat.
   - Add the cooked orzo to the skillet and sauté for 2-3 minutes to heat it through.
5. **Combine and Add Lemon:**

- Add the air-fried shrimp and asparagus to the skillet with the orzo.
- Squeeze the juice of 1 lemon over the mixture and toss to combine.

6. **Serve:**
   - Garnish the Lemon Garlic Shrimp and Asparagus Orzo with fresh parsley leaves.
   - Serve with lemon wedges for additional flavor.

Nutritional Information (per serving):

- Carbs: 40g
- Fats: 8g
- Fiber: 6g
- Protein: 26g

Moroccan Chickpea and Date Tagliatelle

Prep Time: 10 minutes
Cook Time: 15 minutes
Number of Servings: 4

Ingredients:

- 8 ounces whole wheat tagliatelle pasta
- 1 can (15 ounces) chickpeas, drained and rinsed
- 1/2 cup pitted dates, chopped
- 2 tablespoons olive oil
- 1 onion, finely chopped
- 2 cloves garlic, minced
- 1 teaspoon ground cumin
- 1/2 teaspoon ground coriander
- 1/2 teaspoon ground cinnamon
- 1/4 teaspoon ground paprika
- 1/4 teaspoon cayenne pepper (adjust to taste)
- Salt and black pepper to taste
- Fresh cilantro leaves, for garnish
- Lemon wedges, for serving

Instructions:

1. **Cook Tagliatelle:**
   - Cook the whole wheat tagliatelle pasta according to package instructions until al dente. Drain and set aside.

2. **Sauté Onion and Spices:**
   - In a large skillet or frying pan, heat the olive oil over medium heat.
   - Add the finely chopped onion and cook until it becomes translucent, about 3-4 minutes.

- Stir in the minced garlic, ground cumin, ground coriander, ground cinnamon, ground paprika, cayenne pepper, salt, and black pepper. Cook for another 1-2 minutes until fragrant.

3. **Add Chickpeas and Dates:**
   - Add the drained and rinsed chickpeas and chopped pitted dates to the skillet. Stir to combine.

4. **Air Fry Chickpea Mixture:**
   - Preheat your air fryer to 375°F (190°C).
   - Transfer the chickpea and date mixture to the air fryer basket.
   - Air fry for about 8-10 minutes, shaking the basket occasionally, until the chickpeas are slightly crispy.

5. **Combine with Tagliatelle:**
   - In a large mixing bowl, add the air-fried chickpea and date mixture with the cooked tagliatelle pasta. Toss to mix sufficiently.

6. **Serve:**
   - Garnish the Moroccan Chickpea and Date Tagliatelle with fresh cilantro leaves.
   - Serve with lemon wedges for squeezing over the pasta.

Nutritional Information (per serving):

- Carbs: 58g
- Fats: 11g
- Fiber: 9g
- Protein: 11g

Italian Farro and Roasted Vegetable Bowl

Prep Time: 15 minutes
Cook Time: 25 minutes
Number of Servings: 4

Ingredients:

For the Farro and Roasted Vegetables:

- 1 cup pearled farro
- 2 cups low-sodium vegetable broth
- 2 cups mixed vegetables (e.g., bell peppers, zucchini, cherry tomatoes), diced or sliced
- 1 tablespoon olive oil
- 2 cloves garlic, minced
- 1 teaspoon dried Italian seasoning
- Salt and black pepper to taste

For the Balsamic Vinaigrette:

- 2 tablespoons balsamic vinegar
- 1 tablespoon olive oil
- 1 teaspoon Dijon mustard
- 1 teaspoon honey or maple syrup (optional)
- Salt and black pepper to taste

For Serving:

- Fresh basil leaves, for garnish
- Grated Parmesan cheese, for garnish (optional)

Instructions:

1. **Prepare Farro:**

    - Rinse the pearled farro under cold water and drain.
    - In a saucepan, bring the low-sodium vegetable broth to a boil.
    - Add the rinsed farro, reduce heat to a simmer, and cover.
    - Cook for about 20-25 minutes or until the farro is tender and has absorbed most of the liquid.
    - Remove from heat, fluff with a fork, and set aside.

2. **Roast Vegetables:**

    - Preheat your air fryer to 375°F (190°C).
    - In a mixing bowl, add the diced or sliced mixed vegetables with one tablespoon of olive oil, minced garlic, dried Italian seasoning, salt, and black pepper. Toss to coat evenly.
    - Place the seasoned vegetables in the air fryer basket and roast for 10-12 minutes or until tender and slightly caramelized.

3. **Prepare Balsamic Vinaigrette:**

    - In a small bowl, whisk the balsamic vinegar, olive oil, Dijon mustard, honey or maple syrup (if using), salt, and black pepper to make the vinaigrette.

4. **Assemble the Bowl:**

    - Divide the cooked farro and roasted vegetables among four bowls.
    - Drizzle each bowl with the prepared balsamic vinaigrette.

5. **Garnish and Serve:**

    - Garnish the Italian Farro and Roasted Vegetable Bowls with fresh basil leaves and grated Parmesan cheese if desired.

Nutritional Information (per serving):

- Carbs: 50g
- Fats: 8g
- Fiber: 10g
- Protein: 7g

Greek Tzatziki Pasta Salad with Cucumber and Dill

Prep Time: 15 minutes
Cook Time: 10 minutes
Number of Servings: 4

Ingredients:

For the Pasta Salad:

- 8 ounces whole wheat penne pasta
- 1 cucumber, diced
- 1/2 red onion, finely chopped
- 1/2 cup cherry tomatoes, halved
- 1/4 cup Kalamata olives, pitted and sliced
- 2 tablespoons fresh dill, chopped
- 1/4 cup crumbled feta cheese (optional)

For the Tzatziki Dressing:

- 1 cup Greek yogurt (low-fat or non-fat)
- 1/2 cucumber, grated and squeezed to remove excess liquid
- 2 cloves garlic, minced
- 1 tablespoon fresh lemon juice
- 1 tablespoon extra-virgin olive oil
- 1 teaspoon dried oregano
- Salt and black pepper to taste

Instructions:

1. **Cook Pasta:**

   - Cook the whole wheat penne pasta according to package instructions until al dente.
   - Drain and rinse the cooked pasta under cold water to stop the cooking process. Set aside.

2. **Prepare Tzatziki Dressing:**

   - In a bowl, add Greek yogurt, grated and squeezed cucumber, minced garlic, fresh lemon juice, extra-virgin olive oil, dried oregano, salt, and black pepper. Mix sufficiently to make the tzatziki dressing.

3. **Assemble Pasta Salad:**

   - In a large mixing bowl, add the cooked

and cooled penne pasta, diced cucumber, finely chopped red onion, halved cherry tomatoes, sliced Kalamata olives, and chopped fresh dill.

- If using, add the crumbled feta cheese to the salad.

4. **Add Tzatziki Dressing:**
   - Pour the tzatziki dressing over the pasta salad.

5. **Toss and Chill:**
   - Gently toss the Greek Tzatziki Pasta Salad to coat all the ingredients with the dressing.
   - Cover the bowl and refrigerate for at least 30 minutes before serving to allow the flavors to meld.

6. **Serve:**
   - Serve the pasta salad chilled as a refreshing Mediterranean-inspired meal.

Nutritional Information (per serving):

- Carbs: 48g
- Fats: 6g
- Fiber: 6g
- Protein: 12g

Spinach and Ricotta Stuffed Shells with Tomato Sauce

Prep Time: 30 minutes
Cook Time: 25 minutes
Number of Servings: 4

Ingredients:

For the Stuffed Shells:

- 20 jumbo pasta shells
- 2 cups fresh spinach, chopped
- 1 cup low-fat ricotta cheese
- 1/4 cup grated Parmesan cheese
- 1/4 cup finely chopped red onion
- 2 cloves garlic, minced
- 1/2 teaspoon dried oregano
- 1/2 teaspoon dried basil
- Salt and pepper to taste

For the Tomato Sauce:

- 1 can (14 ounces) diced tomatoes
- 1/2 cup tomato sauce
- 2 cloves garlic, minced
- 1/2 teaspoon dried oregano
- 1/2 teaspoon dried basil
- Salt and black pepper to taste

For the Topping:

- 1/4 cup grated Parmesan cheese

- Fresh basil leaves, for garnish

Instructions:

1. **Prepare the Stuffed Shells:**
   - Cook the jumbo pasta shells according to package instructions until al dente. Drain and set aside.

2. **Prepare the Filling:**
   - In a mixing bowl, add chopped fresh spinach, low-fat ricotta cheese, grated Parmesan cheese, finely chopped red onion, minced garlic, dried oregano, dried basil, salt, and pepper. Mix sufficiently.

3. **Stuff the Shells:**
   - Preheat your air fryer to 350°F (175°C).
   - Carefully stuff each cooked pasta shell with the spinach and ricotta mixture, ensuring well-filled but not overflowing.

4. **Prepare the Tomato Sauce:**
   - In a separate bowl, add the diced tomatoes, tomato sauce, minced garlic, dried oregano, dried basil, salt, and black pepper.

5. **Air Fry the Stuffed Shells:**
   - Place the stuffed shells in the air fryer basket in a single layer.
   - Air fry at 350°F (175°C) for 10-12 minutes or until the shells are heated through.

6. **Serve:**
   - Pour the tomato sauce over the air-fried stuffed shells.
   - Sprinkle with grated Parmesan cheese.

7. **Garnish:**
   - Garnish with fresh basil leaves.

Nutritional Information (per serving):

- Carbs: 44g
- Fats: 6g
- Fiber: 5g
- Protein: 15g

Lemon Garlic Spaghetti with Roasted Cherry Tomatoes

Prep Time: 15 minutes
Cook Time: 20 minutes
Number of Servings: 4

Ingredients:

For the Lemon Garlic Spaghetti:

- 8 ounces whole wheat spaghetti
- 2 tablespoons olive oil
- 4 cloves garlic, minced
- Zest of 1 lemon
- Juice of 1 lemon
- 1/2 teaspoon dried red pepper flakes (adjust to taste)
- Salt and black pepper to taste
- 1/4 cup fresh basil leaves, chopped
- 1/4 cup grated Parmesan cheese (optional)

For the Roasted Cherry Tomatoes:

- 2 cups cherry tomatoes
- 1 tablespoon olive oil
- Salt and black pepper to taste

Instructions:

1. **Roast Cherry Tomatoes:**
    - Preheat your air fryer to 375°F (190°C).
    - In a bowl, toss the cherry tomatoes with one tablespoon of olive oil, salt, and black pepper.
    - Place the seasoned tomatoes in the air fryer basket and roast for 10-12 minutes or until blistered and slightly caramelized. Set aside.
2. **Cook Spaghetti:**
    - Cook the whole wheat spaghetti according to package instructions until al dente.
    - Drain and set aside.
3. **Prepare Lemon Garlic Sauce:**
    - In a large skillet or frying pan, heat two tablespoons of olive oil over medium heat.
    - Add the minced garlic and dried red pepper flakes. Sauté for about 1 minute until fragrant.
4. **Combine Spaghetti and Sauce:**
    - Add the cooked and drained whole wheat spaghetti to the skillet with the garlic and red pepper flakes.
    - Stir in the lemon zest and lemon juice.
    - Season with salt and black pepper to taste.
5. **Serve:**
    - Divide the Lemon Garlic Spaghetti among four plates.
    - Top each portion with the roasted cherry tomatoes.
6. **Garnish:**
    - Garnish with chopped fresh basil leaves and

grated Parmesan cheese (if using).

Nutritional Information (per serving):

- Carbs: 35g
- Fats: 8g
- Fiber: 6g
- Protein: 8g

Moroccan Spiced Couscous with Roasted Vegetables

Prep Time: 20 minutes
Cook Time: 20 minutes
Number of Servings: 4

Ingredients:

For the Roasted Vegetables:

- 2 cups mixed vegetables (e.g., bell peppers, zucchini, carrots), diced
- 1 tablespoon olive oil
- 1 teaspoon ground cumin
- 1/2 teaspoon ground coriander
- 1/2 teaspoon ground paprika
- Salt and black pepper to taste

For the Couscous:

- 1 cup whole wheat couscous
- 1 1/4 cups low-sodium vegetable broth
- 1/2 teaspoon ground cumin
- 1/2 teaspoon ground coriander
- 1/2 teaspoon ground cinnamon
- 1/4 teaspoon ground paprika
- Salt and black pepper to taste
- Zest of 1 lemon
- 1/4 cup fresh cilantro leaves, chopped
- 1/4 cup sliced almonds, toasted (optional)

Instructions:

1. **Roast the Vegetables:**
   - Preheat your air fryer to 375°F (190°C).
   - In a bowl, toss the diced mixed vegetables with olive oil, ground cumin, ground coriander, ground paprika, salt, and black pepper.
   - Place the seasoned vegetables in the air fryer basket and roast for 10-12 minutes or until tender and slightly caramelized. Set aside.

2. **Prepare the Couscous:**
   - In a saucepan, bring the low-sodium vegetable broth to a boil.
   - Stir in the whole wheat couscous, ground cumin, ground coriander,

ground cinnamon, ground paprika, salt, and black pepper.

- Cover the saucepan, remove it from heat, and let it sit for about 5 minutes to allow the couscous to absorb the liquid.

3. **Fluff and Season Couscous:**

    - Fluff the cooked couscous with a fork to separate the grains.

    - Stir in the lemon zest and chopped fresh cilantro leaves.

4. **Serve:**

    - Divide the Moroccan Spiced Couscous among four plates.

    - Top each portion with the roasted vegetables.

    - If desired, garnish with toasted sliced almonds.

Nutritional Information (per serving):

- Carbs: 52g
- Fats: 7g
- Fiber: 8g
- Protein: 9g

Italian Brown Rice Risotto with Wild Mushrooms

Prep Time: 15 minutes
Cook Time: 35 minutes
Number of Servings: 4

Ingredients:

For the Risotto:

- 1 cup brown rice
- 2 1/2 cups low-sodium vegetable broth
- 1/2 cup dry white wine (optional)
- 1 cup wild mushrooms, sliced
- 1 small onion, finely chopped
- 2 cloves garlic, minced
- 2 tablespoons olive oil
- 1/2 teaspoon dried thyme
- 1/2 teaspoon dried rosemary
- Salt and black pepper to taste
- 1/4 cup grated Parmesan cheese (optional)

Instructions:

1. **Prepare the Brown Rice:**

    - Rinse the brown rice under cold water and drain.

    - In a saucepan, bring the low-sodium vegetable broth to a simmer.

- Add the rinsed brown rice to the simmering broth, cover, and cook over low heat for about 25-30 minutes or until the rice is tender and most of the liquid is absorbed. Take it out from heat and set aside.

2. **Sauté Mushrooms and Onions:**

   - Preheat your air fryer to 375°F (190°C).
   - In a bowl, toss the sliced wild mushrooms with one tablespoon of olive oil, dried thyme, dried rosemary, salt, and black pepper.
   - Place the seasoned mushrooms in the air fryer basket and roast for 5-7 minutes or until slightly browned and tender. Set aside.

3. **Prepare the Risotto Base:**

   - In a large skillet or frying pan, heat the remaining one tablespoon of olive oil over medium heat.
   - Add the finely chopped onion and cook until it becomes translucent, about 3-4 minutes.
   - Stir in the minced garlic and cook for an extra 30 seconds until fragrant.

4. **Combine Risotto Ingredients:**

   - If using, pour in the dry white wine and stir until it's mostly absorbed by the onions.
   - Add the cooked brown rice to the skillet, followed by the air-fried wild mushrooms. Stir to combine.

5. **Finish and Serve:**

   - Cook for an extra 5 minutes, stirring occasionally, until the risotto is heated through.
   - If desired, stir in the grated Parmesan cheese.
   - Serve the Italian Brown Rice Risotto with Wild Mushrooms hot.

Nutritional Information (per serving):

- Carbs: 38g
- Fats: 8g
- Fiber: 3g
- Protein: 6g

Greek Orzo and Tomato Pilaf

Prep Time: 15 minutes
Cook Time: 20 minutes
Number of Servings: 4

Ingredients:

For the Pilaf:

- 1 cup whole wheat orzo pasta
- 2 cups low-sodium vegetable broth
- 2 cups cherry tomatoes, halved
- 1/2 cup red bell pepper, diced
- 1/2 cup red onion, finely chopped
- 2 cloves garlic, minced
- 2 tablespoons olive oil
- 1 teaspoon dried oregano
- Salt and black pepper to taste
- 1/4 cup fresh parsley leaves, chopped
- Crumbled feta cheese for garnish (optional)

Instructions:

1. **Prepare Orzo:**
   - Rinse the whole wheat orzo pasta under cold water and drain.
   - In a saucepan, bring the low-sodium vegetable broth to a boil.
   - Add the rinsed orzo pasta, reduce heat to a simmer, and cover.
   - Cook for about 10-12 minutes or until the orzo is tender and has absorbed most of the liquid. Take it out from heat and set aside.

2. **Air Fry Cherry Tomatoes:**
   - Preheat your air fryer to 375°F (190°C).
   - In a bowl, toss the halved cherry tomatoes with one tablespoon of olive oil, minced garlic, dried oregano, salt, and black pepper.
   - Place the seasoned tomatoes in the air fryer basket and roast for 5-7 minutes or until slightly caramelized. Set aside.

3. **Sauté Vegetables:**
   - In a large skillet or frying pan, heat the remaining one tablespoon of olive oil over medium heat.
   - Add the diced red bell pepper and finely chopped red onion. Sauté for about 3-4

minutes until they become tender.

4. **Combine Ingredients:**
   - Add the cooked orzo pasta to the skillet with the sautéed vegetables.
   - Gently fold in the air-fried cherry tomatoes.

5. **Finish and Serve:**
   - Cook for an extra 2-3 minutes, stirring occasionally, until everything is heated through.
   - Season with additional salt and black pepper if needed.
   - Garnish the Greek Orzo and Tomato Pilaf with chopped fresh parsley leaves and, if desired, crumbled feta cheese.

Nutritional Information (per serving):

- Carbs: 42g
- Fats: 8g
- Fiber: 6g
- Protein: 6g

Spinach and Ricotta Stuffed Pasta Shells with Marinara

Prep Time: 20 minutes
Cook Time: 25 minutes
Number of Servings: 4

Ingredients:

For the Stuffed Pasta Shells:

- 20 jumbo pasta shells
- 2 cups fresh spinach, chopped
- 1 1/2 cups low-fat ricotta cheese
- 1/4 cup grated Parmesan cheese
- 1/4 cup part-skim mozzarella cheese, shredded
- 1 egg
- 1/2 teaspoon dried basil
- 1/2 teaspoon dried oregano
- Salt and black pepper to taste

For the Marinara Sauce:

- 2 cups canned crushed tomatoes
- 1/2 cup onion, finely chopped
- 2 cloves garlic, minced
- 1/2 teaspoon dried basil
- 1/2 teaspoon dried oregano
- Salt and black pepper to taste

For the Topping:

- 1/4 cup part-skim mozzarella cheese, shredded

- Fresh basil leaves, for garnish (optional)

Instructions:

1. **Prepare the Stuffed Pasta Shells:**
   - Cook the jumbo pasta shells according to package instructions until al dente. Drain and set aside.

2. **Prepare the Filling:**
   - In a mixing bowl, add chopped fresh spinach, low-fat ricotta cheese, grated Parmesan cheese, shredded part-skim mozzarella cheese, egg, dried basil, dried oregano, salt, and black pepper. Mix sufficiently.

3. **Stuff the Shells:**
   - Preheat your air fryer to 350°F (175°C).
   - Carefully stuff each cooked pasta shell with the spinach and ricotta mixture, ensuring well-filled but not overflowing.

4. **Prepare the Marinara Sauce:**
   - In a separate bowl, add the canned crushed tomatoes, finely chopped onion, minced garlic, dried basil, dried oregano, salt, and black pepper to make the marinara sauce.

5. **Air Fry the Stuffed Shells:**
   - Place the stuffed shells in the air fryer basket in a single layer.
   - Air fry at 350°F (175°C) for 10-12 minutes or until the shells are heated through.

6. **Top with Sauce and Cheese:**
   - Spread a small amount of the marinara sauce in the bottom of an oven-safe dish.
   - Arrange the air-fried stuffed shells in the dish.
   - Pour the remaining marinara sauce over the shells.
   - Sprinkle with shredded part-skim mozzarella cheese.

7. **Bake:**
   - Preheat your air fryer to 350°F (175°C) with the air fryer basket removed.
   - Place the dish with the stuffed shells in the preheated air fryer.

- Air fry for 5-7 minutes or until the cheese is bubbly and slightly golden.

8. **Garnish and Serve:**
   - Garnish with fresh basil leaves if desired.
   - Serve the Spinach and Ricotta Stuffed Pasta Shells with Marinara hot.

Nutritional Information (per serving):

- Carbs: 53g
- Fats: 16g
- Fiber: 6g
- Protein: 29g

Lemon Artichoke Linguine with Arugula and Walnuts

Prep Time: 15 minutes
Cook Time: 15 minutes
Number of Servings: 4

Ingredients:

For the Lemon Artichoke Linguine:

- 8 ounces whole wheat linguine
- 1 can (14 ounces) artichoke hearts, drained and quartered
- Zest and juice of 1 lemon
- 2 cloves garlic, minced
- 2 tablespoons extra-virgin olive oil
- 1/4 cup chopped fresh parsley
- Salt and black pepper to taste

For the Arugula and Walnut Topping:

- 2 cups fresh arugula leaves
- 1/4 cup walnuts, chopped
- 1 tablespoon extra-virgin olive oil
- 1 tablespoon lemon juice
- Salt and black pepper to taste

Instructions:

1. **Cook Linguine:**
   - Cook the whole wheat linguine according to package instructions until al dente. Drain and set aside.

2. **Prepare Lemon Artichoke Sauce:**
   - In a large skillet or frying pan, heat two tablespoons of extra-virgin olive oil over medium heat.
   - Add the minced garlic and sauté for about 1 minute until fragrant.
   - Stir in the quartered artichoke hearts, lemon zest, and lemon juice.

- Cook for an extra 2-3 minutes until the artichokes are heated through.

3. **Combine Linguine and Artichoke Sauce:**

    - Add the cooked whole wheat linguine to the skillet with the lemon artichoke sauce.
    - Toss to combine and coat the pasta evenly.
    - Stir in the chopped fresh parsley.
    - Season with salt and black pepper to taste.

4. **Prepare Arugula and Walnut Topping:**

    - In a separate bowl, add the fresh arugula leaves, chopped walnuts, one tablespoon of extra-virgin olive oil, and one tablespoon of lemon juice.
    - Toss to coat the arugula and walnuts evenly.
    - Season with salt and black pepper to taste.

5. **Serve:**

    - Divide the Lemon Artichoke Linguine among four plates.
    - Top each portion with the arugula and walnut topping.

Nutritional Information (per serving):

- Carbs: 38g
- Fats: 15g
- Fiber: 8g
- Protein: 9g

Greek-style Orzo Risotto with Sundried Tomatoes

Prep Time: 10 minutes
Cook Time: 20 minutes
Number of Servings: 4

Ingredients:

For the Orzo Risotto:

- 1 cup whole wheat orzo pasta
- 2 cups low-sodium vegetable broth
- 1/2 cup sundried tomatoes, chopped
- 1/2 cup Kalamata olives, pitted and sliced
- 1/4 cup red onion, finely chopped
- 2 cloves garlic, minced
- 2 tablespoons extra-virgin olive oil
- 1/2 teaspoon dried oregano
- Salt and black pepper to taste
- 1/4 cup crumbled feta cheese (optional)

For the Topping:

- Fresh parsley leaves, chopped, for garnish (optional)
- Lemon wedges, for garnish (optional)

Instructions:

1. **Cook Orzo Risotto:**
    - Rinse the whole wheat orzo pasta under cold water and drain.
    - In a saucepan, bring the low-sodium vegetable broth to a boil.
    - Add the rinsed orzo pasta to the simmering broth, cover, and cook over low heat for about 10-12 minutes or until the orzo is tender and has absorbed most of the liquid. Take it out from heat and set aside.
2. **Sauté Vegetables:**
    - In a large skillet or frying pan, heat two tablespoons of extra-virgin olive oil over medium heat.
    - Add the finely chopped red onion and minced garlic. Sauté for about 3-4 minutes until the onion becomes translucent.
3. **Combine Orzo and Vegetables:**
    - Add the cooked orzo pasta to the skillet with the sautéed red onion and garlic.
    - Stir in the chopped sundried tomatoes and sliced Kalamata olives.
    - Add the dried oregano.
    - Season with salt and black pepper to taste.
4. **Finish and Serve:**
    - Cook for an extra 2-3 minutes, stirring occasionally, until everything is heated through.
    - If desired, sprinkle crumbled feta cheese over the Greek-style Orzo Risotto.
    - Garnish with chopped fresh parsley leaves and lemon wedges if desired.

Nutritional Information (per serving):

- Carbs: 38g
- Fats: 9g
- Fiber: 6g
- Protein: 7g

Moroccan Couscous Pilaf with Apricots and Almonds

Prep Time: 15 minutes
Cook Time: 15 minutes
Number of Servings: 4

Ingredients:

For the Couscous Pilaf:

- 1 cup whole wheat couscous
- 1 1/4 cups low-sodium vegetable broth
- 1/2 cup dried apricots, chopped
- 1/4 cup slivered almonds, toasted
- 1/4 cup red onion, finely chopped
- 2 cloves garlic, minced
- 2 tablespoons olive oil
- 1/2 teaspoon ground cumin
- 1/2 teaspoon ground coriander
- 1/4 teaspoon ground cinnamon
- Salt and black pepper to taste

For the Topping:

- Fresh cilantro leaves, chopped, for garnish (optional)
- Lemon wedges, for garnish (optional)

Instructions:

1. **Prepare Couscous:**
   - In a saucepan, bring the low-sodium vegetable broth to a boil.
   - Stir in the whole wheat couscous, cover the saucepan, and remove it from heat.
   - Let it sit for about 5 minutes to allow the couscous to absorb the liquid.

2. **Sauté Onions and Garlic:**
   - In a large skillet or frying pan, heat two tablespoons of olive oil over medium heat.
   - Add the finely chopped red onion and minced garlic. Sauté for about 3-4 minutes until the onion becomes translucent.

3. **Add Spices and Couscous:**
   - Stir in the ground cumin, ground coriander, and ground cinnamon into the sautéed onions and garlic.
   - Add the cooked whole wheat couscous to the skillet and toss to combine with the spices and onions.
   - Season with salt and black pepper to taste.

4. **Fold in Apricots and Almonds:**
   - Add the chopped dried apricots and toasted slivered almonds to the couscous mixture.
   - Gently fold everything together.
5. **Finish and Serve:**
   - Cook for an extra 2-3 minutes, stirring occasionally, until everything is heated through.
   - If desired, garnish the Moroccan Couscous Pilaf with chopped fresh cilantro leaves and serve with lemon wedges on the side.

Nutritional Information (per serving):

- Carbs: 47g
- Fats: 13g
- Fiber: 7g
- Protein: 7g

Mediterranean Spaghetti Squash with Roasted Red Pepper Sauce

Prep Time: 15 minutes
Cook Time: 40 minutes
Number of Servings: 4

Ingredients:

For the Spaghetti Squash:

- 1 medium spaghetti squash
- 1 tablespoon olive oil
- Salt and black pepper to taste

For the Roasted Red Pepper Sauce:

- 2 red bell peppers, roasted, peeled, and seeded
- 2 cloves garlic, minced
- 1/4 cup tomato paste
- 2 tablespoons extra-virgin olive oil
- 1 teaspoon dried basil
- 1 teaspoon dried oregano
- Salt and black pepper to taste

For Topping and Garnish:

- 1/4 cup fresh basil leaves, chopped
- 1/4 cup crumbled feta cheese (optional)

Instructions:

1. **Prepare Spaghetti Squash:**
   - Preheat your air fryer to 375°F (190°C).
   - Cut the spaghetti squash in half lengthwise and scoop out the seeds.
   - Brush the cut sides of the squash with one tablespoon of olive oil.

- Season with salt and black pepper.
- Place the squash halves, cut side down, in the air fryer basket.
- Air fry for 20-25 minutes or until the squash is tender and easily separates into spaghetti-like strands with a fork.
- Once done, use a fork to scrape the strands of cooked squash. Set aside.

2. **Prepare Roasted Red Pepper Sauce:**
   - In a blender or food processor, add the roasted red bell peppers, minced garlic, tomato paste, extra-virgin olive oil, dried basil, dried oregano, salt, and black pepper.
   - Blend until the sauce is smooth and well combined.

3. **Warm the Sauce:**
   - Transfer the red pepper sauce to a saucepan and warm it over low heat for about 5 minutes, stirring occasionally.

4. **Combine Squash and Sauce:**
   - In a large mixing bowl, toss the cooked spaghetti squash strands with the roasted red pepper sauce until well coated.

5. **Serve:**
   - Divide the Mediterranean Spaghetti Squash with Roasted Red Pepper Sauce among four plates.
   - If desired, garnish with chopped fresh basil leaves and crumbled feta cheese.

Nutritional Information (per serving):

- Carbs: 16g
- Fats: 9g
- Fiber: 3g
- Protein: 2g

LEGUMES AND BEANS

Spanish White Bean and Chorizo Stew

Prep Time: 15 minutes
Cook Time: 25 minutes
Number of Servings: 4

Ingredients:

- 1 lb (450g) lean turkey chorizo sausage, sliced
- 1 onion, diced
- 2 cloves garlic, minced
- 2 cups low-sodium chicken broth
- 2 cans (15 oz each) white beans, drained and rinsed
- 1 can (14.5 oz) diced tomatoes
- 1 teaspoon smoked paprika
- 1/2 teaspoon cumin
- 1/2 teaspoon dried oregano
- Salt and pepper to taste
- 1 bay leaf
- 1 cup chopped kale, stems removed
- 2 tablespoons fresh parsley, chopped
- 1 tablespoon olive oil

Instructions:

1. In a large air fryer-safe skillet, heat the olive oil over medium heat. Add the diced onion and cook for about 3 minutes, or until it becomes translucent.
2. Add the sliced turkey chorizo sausage to the skillet and cook for an extra 3-4 minutes, or until it starts to brown.
3. Stir in the minced garlic, smoked paprika, cumin, and dried oregano. Cook for 1-2 minutes until the spices are fragrant.
4. Pour in the low-sodium chicken broth, diced tomatoes, drained and rinsed white beans, bay leaf, salt, and pepper. Stir to combine all the ingredients.
5. Transfer the skillet to the air fryer basket and set the air fryer to 350°F (180°C). Cook for 15-20 minutes, or until the stew is bubbling and the flavors have melded together. Make sure to stir the stew occasionally to prevent sticking.
6. When the stew is almost done, stir in the chopped kale and continue cooking for an extra 2-3 minutes, or until the kale wilts.
7. Once the stew is ready, take out the bay leaf and discard it.

8. Serve the Spanish White Bean and Chorizo Stew hot, garnished with chopped fresh parsley.

Nutritional Information (per serving):

- Carbs: 30g
- Fats: 9g
- Fiber: 8g
- Protein: 23g

Italian-Style Lentil Salad with Sun-Dried Tomatoes

Prep Time: 10 minutes
Cook Time: 25 minutes
Number of Servings: 4

Ingredients:

- 1 cup green or brown lentils
- 2 cups water
- 1/2 cup sun-dried tomatoes (not in oil), thinly sliced
- 1/4 cup red onion, finely diced
- 2 cloves garlic, minced
- 1/4 cup fresh basil leaves, chopped
- 1/4 cup fresh parsley leaves, chopped
- 2 tablespoons balsamic vinegar
- 1 tablespoon olive oil
- Salt and pepper to taste
- 1/4 cup crumbled feta cheese (optional, for garnish)

Instructions:

1. Rinse the lentils thoroughly under cold water and drain.

2. In an air fryer-safe pot, add the rinsed lentils and two cups of water. Place the pot in the air fryer basket and set the air fryer to 375°F (190°C). Cook for 20-25 minutes, or until the lentils are tender but still firm (al dente). Drain any excess water and let the lentils cool.

3. In a large mixing bowl, add the cooked lentils, sliced sun-dried tomatoes, finely diced red onion, minced garlic, chopped basil, and chopped parsley.

4. In a separate small bowl, whisk the balsamic vinegar and olive oil. Pour this dressing over the lentil mixture and toss to coat evenly. Season with salt and pepper to taste.

5. If desired, garnish the Italian-Style Lentil Salad with crumbled feta cheese.

6. Serve the salad immediately, or refrigerate it for a few hours to allow the flavors to meld.

Nutritional Information (per serving, without feta cheese):

- Carbs: 31g

- Fats: 4g
- Fiber: 12g
- Protein: 14g

Greek Gigantes Plaki (Baked Giant Beans)

Prep Time: 15 minutes
Cook Time: 25 minutes
Number of Servings: 4

Ingredients:

- 1 cup dried giant white beans
- 4 cups water
- 1 onion, finely diced
- 2 cloves garlic, minced
- 1 can (14.5 oz) diced tomatoes
- 1/4 cup fresh parsley, chopped
- 2 tablespoons olive oil
- 1 teaspoon dried oregano
- 1 teaspoon ground cumin
- Salt and pepper to taste
- 1/4 cup crumbled feta cheese (optional, for garnish)

Instructions:

1. Rinse the dried giant white beans under cold water and drain.
2. In an air fryer-safe pot, add the rinsed beans and 4 cups of water. Place the pot in the air fryer basket and set the air fryer to 375°F (190°C). Cook for 20-25 minutes, or until the beans are tender but not mushy. Drain any excess water and set the beans aside.
3. In another air fryer-safe skillet, heat the olive oil over medium heat. Add the finely diced onion and cook for about 3 minutes until it becomes translucent.
4. Stir in the minced garlic, dried oregano, and ground cumin. Cook for an extra 1-2 minutes until the spices are fragrant.
5. Add the canned diced tomatoes to the skillet and cook for another 5 minutes, allowing the mixture to simmer and thicken slightly.
6. Add the cooked giant white beans to the tomato mixture in the skillet. Stir to combine, ensuring the beans are well coated with the tomato sauce.
7. Transfer the skillet to the air fryer basket and set the air fryer to 350°F (180°C). Cook for an extra 10 minutes to meld the flavors, stirring occasionally.
8. Season the Gigantes Plaki with salt and pepper to taste.
9. Serve the dish hot, garnished with chopped fresh parsley and crumbled feta cheese (optional).

Nutritional Information (per serving, without feta cheese):

- Carbs: 36g
- Fats: 7g
- Fiber: 10g
- Protein: 10g

Chickpea and Artichoke Tagine

Prep Time: 15 minutes
Cook Time: 25 minutes
Number of Servings: 4

Ingredients:

- 2 cups canned chickpeas, drained and rinsed
- 1 can (14 oz) artichoke hearts, drained and quartered
- 1 onion, finely diced
- 2 cloves garlic, minced
- 1 can (14.5 oz) diced tomatoes
- 1/2 cup vegetable broth
- 1 teaspoon ground cumin
- 1/2 teaspoon ground coriander
- 1/2 teaspoon ground paprika
- 1/2 teaspoon ground cinnamon
- Salt and pepper to taste
- 2 tablespoons fresh cilantro, chopped
- 2 tablespoons olive oil

Instructions:

1. In an air fryer-safe skillet, heat the olive oil over medium heat. Add the finely diced onion and cook for about 3 minutes, or until it becomes translucent.
2. Stir in the minced garlic, ground cumin, ground coriander, ground paprika, and ground cinnamon. Cook for an extra 1-2 minutes until the spices are fragrant.
3. Add the drained and rinsed chickpeas, quartered artichoke hearts, canned diced tomatoes, and vegetable broth to the skillet. Stir to combine all the ingredients.
4. Transfer the skillet to the air fryer basket and set the air fryer to 350°F (180°C). Cook for 20-25 minutes, or until the tagine is heated through and the flavors have melded together. Stir occasionally to prevent sticking.
5. Season the Chickpea and Artichoke Tagine with salt and pepper to taste.
6. Serve the tagine hot, garnished with chopped fresh cilantro.

Nutritional Information (per serving):

- Carbs: 35g
- Fats: 7g

- Fiber: 11g
- Protein: 10g

Tuscan White Bean and Rosemary Hummus

Prep Time: 10 minutes
Cook Time: 5 minutes
Number of Servings: 4

Ingredients:

- 2 cups canned white beans (cannellini or Great Northern), drained and rinsed
- 2 cloves garlic, minced
- 2 tablespoons fresh rosemary leaves, chopped
- 2 tablespoons olive oil
- 1 lemon, juiced and zested
- Salt and pepper to taste
- 1/4 cup water (for desired consistency)
- 1 tablespoon pine nuts, toasted (optional, for garnish)
- Fresh rosemary sprigs (optional, for garnish)

Instructions:

1. In an air fryer-safe skillet, heat one tablespoon of olive oil over medium heat. Add the minced garlic and chopped fresh rosemary. Sauté for about 1-2 minutes, or until the garlic becomes fragrant and the rosemary is slightly crispy. Take it out from heat and let it cool.
2. In a food processor, add the drained and rinsed white beans, the sautéed garlic and rosemary mixture, lemon juice, and lemon zest.
3. Process the mixture until it starts to form a thick paste. Add water as needed to achieve your desired hummus consistency.
4. While the food processor is running, drizzle in the remaining one tablespoon of olive oil and continue to blend until the hummus is smooth and creamy.
5. Season the Tuscan White Bean and Rosemary Hummus with salt and pepper to taste. Adjust the lemon juice or rosemary if desired.
6. Transfer the hummus to a serving dish and garnish with toasted pine nuts and fresh rosemary sprigs if you like.

Nutritional Information (per serving, without optional garnishes):

- Carbs: 26g
- Fats: 7g
- Fiber: 7g
- Protein: 8g

Lebanese Mujadara with Quinoa

Prep Time: 15 minutes
Cook Time: 25 minutes
Number of Servings: 4

Ingredients:

- 1 cup quinoa, rinsed and drained
- 1/2 cup brown lentils, rinsed and drained
- 1 large onion, thinly sliced
- 3 tablespoons olive oil
- 1 teaspoon ground cumin
- 1 teaspoon ground coriander
- Salt and pepper to taste
- 2 cups water
- Fresh parsley, chopped (for garnish)

Instructions:

1. In an air fryer-safe pot, heat two tablespoons of olive oil over medium heat. Add the thinly sliced onion and sauté until golden brown and crispy. Remove half of the cooked onions and set aside for garnishing.
2. Add the rinsed quinoa and brown lentils to the pot with the remaining sautéed onions. Stir in the ground cumin, ground coriander, salt, and pepper. Cook for 2-3 minutes to toast the quinoa and lentils, stirring occasionally.
3. Pour in two cups of water and bring the mixture to a boil. Reduce the heat to low, cover, and simmer for 15-20 minutes or until the quinoa and lentils are cooked and the water is absorbed. Take it out from heat and let it rest for 5 minutes.
4. While the quinoa and lentils are resting, in a separate air fryer-safe skillet, heat the remaining one tablespoon of olive oil. Add the reserved crispy onions and sauté briefly until warmed.
5. Serve the Mujadara hot, garnished with the sautéed crispy onions and chopped fresh parsley.

Nutritional Information (per serving):

- Carbs: 50g
- Fats: 11g
- Fiber: 12g
- Protein: 14g

Italian Cannellini Bean and Escarole Soup

Prep Time: 15 minutes
Cook Time: 25 minutes
Number of Servings: 4

Ingredients:

- 2 cups canned cannellini beans, drained and rinsed
- 1 head escarole, washed and chopped

- 1 onion, finely diced
- 2 cloves garlic, minced
- 1 can (14.5 oz) diced tomatoes
- 4 cups low-sodium vegetable broth
- 2 tablespoons olive oil
- 1 teaspoon dried oregano
- 1/2 teaspoon dried thyme
- Salt and pepper to taste
- Grated Parmesan cheese (optional, for garnish)

Instructions:

1. In an air fryer-safe pot, heat the olive oil over medium heat. Add the finely diced onion and cook for about 3 minutes, or until it becomes translucent.
2. Stir in the minced garlic, dried oregano, and dried thyme. Cook for an extra 1-2 minutes until the spices are fragrant.
3. Add the washed and chopped escarole to the pot. Sauté for 2-3 minutes, or until the escarole wilts.
4. Pour in the canned diced tomatoes, canned cannellini beans, and low-sodium vegetable broth. Stir to combine all the ingredients.
5. Transfer the pot to the air fryer basket and set the air fryer to 350°F (180°C). Cook for 20-25 minutes, or until the soup is heated through and the flavors have melded together. Stir occasionally to prevent sticking.
6. Season the Cannellini Bean and Escarole Soup with salt and pepper to taste.
7. Serve the soup hot, garnished with grated Parmesan cheese if desired.

Nutritional Information (per serving, without Parmesan cheese):

- Carbs: 38g
- Fats: 7g
- Fiber: 13g
- Protein: 12g

Harissa Spiced Lentil Tacos

Prep Time: 15 minutes
Cook Time: 25 minutes
Number of Servings: 4

Ingredients:

For the Harissa Spiced Lentils:

- 1 cup dried brown lentils, rinsed and drained
- 2 cups vegetable broth
- 1 onion, finely diced
- 2 cloves garlic, minced
- 2 tablespoons harissa paste
- 1 teaspoon ground cumin
- 1/2 teaspoon ground coriander

- Salt and pepper to taste
- 1 tablespoon olive oil

For Assembling Tacos:

- 8 small whole-grain or corn tortillas
- 1 cup Greek yogurt (low-fat, if desired)
- 1 cup fresh cucumber, diced
- 1 cup fresh tomatoes, diced
- 1/2 cup fresh cilantro, chopped
- 1/4 cup red onion, finely diced
- 1 lemon, cut into wedges

Instructions:

For the Harissa Spiced Lentils:

1. In an air fryer-safe pot, heat the olive oil over medium heat. Add the finely diced onion and cook for about 3 minutes, or until it becomes translucent.
2. Stir in the minced garlic, harissa paste, ground cumin, and ground coriander. Cook for an extra 1-2 minutes until the spices are fragrant.
3. Add the rinsed brown lentils and vegetable broth to the pot. Bring to a boil, then reduce the heat to low, cover, and simmer for 20-25 minutes, or until the lentils are tender and the liquid is absorbed. Stir occasionally.
4. Season the Harissa Spiced Lentils with salt and pepper to taste.

For Assembling Tacos:

1. Warm the whole-grain or corn tortillas in the air fryer for a few seconds until pliable.
2. To assemble each taco, spoon a generous portion of the Harissa Spiced Lentils onto a tortilla.
3. Top with Greek yogurt, diced cucumber, diced tomatoes, chopped cilantro, and finely diced red onion.
4. Squeeze fresh lemon juice from lemon wedges over the taco before serving.

Nutritional Information (per serving, for one taco with toppings):

- Carbs: 43g
- Fats: 8g
- Fiber: 12g
- Protein: 15g

Greek-Style Butter Beans with Tomato and Dill

Prep Time: 15 minutes
Cook Time: 25 minutes
Number of Servings: 4

Ingredients:

- 2 cups canned butter beans, drained and rinsed

- 1 onion, finely diced
- 2 cloves garlic, minced
- 1 can (14.5 oz) diced tomatoes
- 1/4 cup fresh dill, chopped
- 2 tablespoons olive oil
- 1 teaspoon dried oregano
- Salt and pepper to taste
- Lemon wedges (for garnish)

Instructions:

1. In an air fryer-safe skillet, heat the olive oil over medium heat. Add the finely diced onion and cook for about 3 minutes, or until it becomes translucent.
2. Stir in the minced garlic and dried oregano. Cook for an extra 1-2 minutes until the garlic is fragrant.
3. Add the canned diced tomatoes and drained butter beans to the skillet. Stir to combine all the ingredients.
4. Transfer the skillet to the air fryer basket and set the air fryer to 350°F (180°C). Cook for 20-25 minutes, or until the dish is heated through and the flavors have melded together. Stir occasionally to prevent sticking.
5. Season the Greek-Style Butter Beans with salt and pepper to taste.
6. Before serving, sprinkle the chopped fresh dill over the beans and garnish with lemon wedges.

Nutritional Information (per serving):

- Carbs: 32g
- Fats: 7g
- Fiber: 9g
- Protein: 7g

Italian White Bean and Escarole Salad with Lemon-Dijon Dressing

Prep Time: 15 minutes
Cook Time: 5 minutes (for toasting pine nuts, optional)
Number of Servings: 4

Ingredients:

For the Salad:

- 2 cans (15 oz each) white beans (cannellini or Great Northern), drained and rinsed
- 1 head escarole, washed and chopped
- 1/4 cup red onion, finely diced
- 1/4 cup fresh parsley, chopped
- 1/4 cup pine nuts, toasted (optional, for garnish)

For the Lemon-Dijon Dressing:

- 1/4 cup olive oil

- 2 tablespoons fresh lemon juice
- 1 teaspoon Dijon mustard
- 1 clove garlic, minced
- Salt and pepper to taste

Instructions:

For the Salad:

1. In an air fryer-safe skillet, toast the pine nuts over medium heat in the air fryer for about 2-3 minutes, or until they turn golden brown. This step is optional but adds a nice crunch to the salad. Set aside to cool.
2. In a large bowl, add the drained and rinsed white beans, washed and chopped escarole, finely diced red onion, and chopped fresh parsley.

For the Lemon-Dijon Dressing:

1. In a separate bowl, whisk the olive oil, fresh lemon juice, Dijon mustard, minced garlic, salt, and pepper until well combined.
2. Pour the Lemon-Dijon Dressing over the salad ingredients in the large bowl.
3. Toss everything together to ensure the salad is well coated with the dressing.
4. If using, sprinkle the toasted pine nuts over the salad as a garnish.

Nutritional Information (per serving, without pine nuts):

- Carbs: 28g
- Fats: 11g
- Fiber: 7g
- Protein: 8g

Spanish Chickpea and Chorizo Stew

Prep Time: 15 minutes
Cook Time: 25 minutes
Number of Servings: 4

Ingredients:

- 1 lb (450g) lean turkey chorizo sausage, sliced
- 1 onion, diced
- 2 cloves garlic, minced
- 2 cups low-sodium chicken broth
- 2 cans (15 oz each) chickpeas, drained and rinsed
- 1 can (14.5 oz) diced tomatoes
- 1 teaspoon smoked paprika
- 1/2 teaspoon cumin
- 1/2 teaspoon dried oregano
- Salt and pepper to taste
- 1 bay leaf
- 1 cup chopped kale, stems removed
- 2 tablespoons fresh parsley, chopped

- 1 tablespoon olive oil

Instructions:

1. In an air fryer-safe skillet, heat the olive oil over medium heat. Add the diced onion and cook for about 3 minutes, or until it becomes translucent.

2. Add the sliced turkey chorizo sausage to the skillet and cook for an extra 3-4 minutes, or until it starts to brown.

3. Stir in the minced garlic, smoked paprika, cumin, and dried oregano. Cook for 1-2 minutes until the spices are fragrant.

4. Pour in the low-sodium chicken broth, diced tomatoes, drained and rinsed chickpeas, bay leaf, salt, and pepper. Stir to combine all the ingredients.

5. Transfer the skillet to the air fryer basket and set the air fryer to 350°F (180°C). Cook for 15-20 minutes, or until the stew is bubbling and the flavors have melded together. Make sure to stir the stew occasionally to prevent sticking.

6. When the stew is almost done, stir in the chopped kale and continue cooking for an extra 2-3 minutes, or until the kale wilts.

7. Once the stew is ready, take out the bay leaf and discard it.

8. Serve the Spanish Chickpea and Chorizo Stew hot, garnished with chopped fresh parsley.

Nutritional Information (per serving):

- Carbs: 31g
- Fats: 9g
- Fiber: 8g
- Protein: 23g

Mediterranean Lentil and Eggplant Casserole

Prep Time: 20 minutes
Cook Time: 40 minutes
Number of Servings: 4

Ingredients:

- 1 cup dried green or brown lentils
- 2 cups water
- 1 large eggplant, sliced into rounds
- 2 tablespoons olive oil
- 1 onion, finely diced
- 2 cloves garlic, minced
- 1 can (14.5 oz) diced tomatoes
- 1/2 cup tomato sauce
- 1 teaspoon dried oregano
- 1 teaspoon dried basil

- Salt and pepper to taste
- 1/4 cup fresh parsley, chopped
- 1/4 cup crumbled feta cheese (optional, for garnish)

Instructions:

1. In an air fryer-safe pot, add the dried lentils and two cups of water. Place the pot in the air fryer basket and set the air fryer to 375°F (190°C). Cook for 20-25 minutes, or until the lentils are tender but still firm (al dente). Drain any excess water and set the lentils aside.

2. While the lentils are cooking, preheat your air fryer to 375°F (190°C). Brush the eggplant slices with olive oil and arrange them in a single layer in the air fryer basket. Cook for about 10-12 minutes, flipping the slices halfway through, until tender and lightly browned. Take out the eggplant from the air fryer and set aside.

3. In an air fryer-safe skillet, heat the remaining olive oil over medium heat. Add the finely diced onion and cook for about 3 minutes, or until it becomes translucent.

4. Stir in the minced garlic and cook for an extra 1-2 minutes until fragrant.

5. Add the canned diced tomatoes, tomato sauce, dried oregano, dried basil, salt, and pepper to the skillet. Cook for 5-7 minutes, allowing the mixture to simmer and thicken slightly.

6. Preheat your air fryer to 375°F (190°C) again.

7. In a casserole dish that fits inside your air fryer, layer the cooked lentils, eggplant slices, and tomato mixture. Repeat the layers as needed.

8. Place the casserole dish in the air fryer basket and cook for 15-20 minutes, or until the casserole is heated through.

9. Garnish the Mediterranean Lentil and Eggplant Casserole with chopped fresh parsley and crumbled feta cheese if desired.

Nutritional Information (per serving, without feta cheese):

- Carbs: 45g
- Fats: 7g
- Fiber: 15g
- Protein: 15g

Harissa Spiced Chickpea and Spinach Saute

Prep Time: 10 minutes
Cook Time: 15 minutes
Number of Servings: 4

Ingredients:

- 2 cans (15 oz each) chickpeas, drained and rinsed
- 8 cups fresh spinach leaves
- 1 onion, finely diced
- 2 cloves garlic, minced
- 2 tablespoons olive oil
- 2 teaspoons harissa paste
- 1 teaspoon ground cumin
- 1/2 teaspoon ground coriander
- Salt and pepper to taste
- Lemon wedges (for garnish)

Instructions:

1. Preheat your air fryer to 375°F (190°C).
2. In an air fryer-safe skillet, heat the olive oil over medium heat. Add the finely diced onion and cook for about 3 minutes, or until it becomes translucent.
3. Stir in the minced garlic, harissa paste, ground cumin, and ground coriander. Cook for an extra 1-2 minutes until the spices are fragrant.
4. Add the drained and rinsed chickpeas to the skillet. Stir to combine with the onion and spices.
5. Transfer the skillet to the air fryer basket and cook for 10-12 minutes, stirring occasionally, until the chickpeas are heated through and slightly crispy.
6. Take out the skillet from the air fryer and stir in the fresh spinach leaves. Let the residual heat wilt the spinach for a minute or two.
7. Season the Harissa Spiced Chickpea and Spinach Saute with salt and pepper to taste.
8. Serve the saute hot, garnished with lemon wedges for an extra burst of flavor.

Nutritional Information (per serving):

- Carbs: 36g
- Fats: 9g
- Fiber: 10g
- Protein: 10g

Greek-Style Gigantes Beans with Tomato and Parsley

Prep Time: 15 minutes
Cook Time: 40 minutes
Number of Servings: 4

Ingredients:

- 2 cups dried gigantes beans (large white beans), soaked overnight
- 1 onion, finely diced
- 2 cloves garlic, minced
- 1 can (14.5 oz) diced tomatoes

- 1/4 cup fresh parsley, chopped
- 2 tablespoons olive oil
- 1 teaspoon dried oregano
- Salt and pepper to taste
- Lemon wedges (for garnish)

Instructions:

1. Preheat your air fryer to 375°F (190°C).
2. In an air fryer-safe pot, heat the olive oil over medium heat. Add the finely diced onion and cook for about 3 minutes, or until it becomes translucent.
3. Stir in the minced garlic and cook for an extra 1-2 minutes until fragrant.
4. Add the soaked and drained gigantes beans to the pot, along with the canned diced tomatoes, dried oregano, salt, and pepper. Stir to combine all the ingredients.
5. Transfer the pot to the air fryer basket and cook for 35-40 minutes, or until the beans are tender and the flavors have melded together. Stir occasionally to prevent sticking.
6. Once the Gigantes Beans are ready, garnish with chopped fresh parsley and serve hot with lemon wedges on the side.

Nutritional Information (per serving):

- Carbs: 47g
- Fats: 7g
- Fiber: 12g
- Protein: 13g

Italian Lentil and Mushroom Stuffed Bell Peppers

Prep Time: 20 minutes
Cook Time: 30 minutes
Number of Servings: 4

Ingredients:

- 4 large bell peppers (red, green, or yellow)
- 1 cup dried green or brown lentils, rinsed and drained
- 2 cups low-sodium vegetable broth
- 1 cup mushrooms, finely diced
- 1 onion, finely diced
- 2 cloves garlic, minced
- 1 can (14.5 oz) diced tomatoes
- 1/2 cup whole-grain breadcrumbs
- 1/4 cup fresh parsley, chopped
- 2 tablespoons olive oil
- 1 teaspoon dried basil
- 1 teaspoon dried oregano
- Salt and pepper to taste

- Grated Parmesan cheese (optional, for garnish)

Instructions:

1. Preheat your air fryer to 375°F (190°C).
2. Cut the tops off the bell peppers and take out the seeds and membranes. Set aside.
3. In an air fryer-safe skillet, heat one tablespoon of olive oil over medium heat. Add the finely diced onion and cook for about 3 minutes, or until it becomes translucent.
4. Stir in the minced garlic and cook for an extra 1-2 minutes until fragrant.
5. Add the diced mushrooms to the skillet and cook for 5-7 minutes, or until they release their moisture and become tender. Take it out from heat and set aside.
6. In a separate pot, add the rinsed lentils and low-sodium vegetable broth. Bring to a boil, then reduce the heat to low, cover, and simmer for 20-25 minutes, or until the lentils are tender but not mushy. Drain any excess liquid.
7. In a large bowl, add the cooked lentils, cooked mushroom and onion mixture, diced tomatoes, whole-grain breadcrumbs, chopped fresh parsley, dried basil, dried oregano, salt, and pepper. Mix everything together thoroughly.
8. Stuff each bell pepper with the lentil and mushroom mixture, pressing it down gently to pack the filling.
9. Place the stuffed bell peppers in the air fryer basket and cook for 25-30 minutes, or until the peppers are tender and slightly charred on the outside.
10. Garnish with grated Parmesan cheese if desired before serving.

Nutritional Information (per serving, without Parmesan cheese):

- Carbs: 45g
- Fats: 7g
- Fiber: 14g
- Protein: 15g

Greek-Style Black-Eyed Peas with Spinach and Tomatoes

Prep Time: 15 minutes
Cook Time: 30 minutes
Number of Servings: 4

Ingredients:

- 2 cups dried black-eyed peas, soaked overnight and drained
- 8 cups fresh spinach leaves
- 1 onion, finely diced

- 2 cloves garlic, minced
- 1 can (14.5 oz) diced tomatoes
- 1/4 cup fresh parsley, chopped
- 2 tablespoons olive oil
- 1 teaspoon dried oregano
- Salt and pepper to taste
- Lemon wedges (for garnish)

Instructions:

1. Preheat your air fryer to 375°F (190°C).
2. In an air fryer-safe pot, heat the olive oil over medium heat. Add the finely diced onion and cook for about 3 minutes, or until it becomes translucent.
3. Stir in the minced garlic and cook for an extra 1-2 minutes until fragrant.
4. Add the soaked and drained black-eyed peas to the pot, along with the canned diced tomatoes, dried oregano, salt, and pepper. Stir to combine all the ingredients.
5. Transfer the pot to the air fryer basket and cook for 25-30 minutes, or until the black-eyed peas are tender and the flavors have melded together. Stir occasionally to prevent sticking.
6. Once the Black-Eyed Peas are ready, stir in the fresh spinach leaves and let the residual heat wilt the spinach for a minute or two.
7. Garnish with chopped fresh parsley and serve hot with lemon wedges on the side.

Nutritional Information (per serving):

- Carbs: 44g
- Fats: 7g
- Fiber: 12g
- Protein: 15g

Moroccan Chickpea and Carrot Tagine

Prep Time: 20 minutes
Cook Time: 30 minutes
Number of Servings: 4

Ingredients:

- 2 cups canned chickpeas, drained and rinsed
- 4 large carrots, peeled and sliced into rounds
- 1 onion, finely diced
- 2 cloves garlic, minced
- 1 can (14.5 oz) diced tomatoes
- 1/2 cup low-sodium vegetable broth
- 2 tablespoons olive oil
- 1 teaspoon ground cumin
- 1 teaspoon ground coriander
- 1/2 teaspoon ground cinnamon

- 1/4 teaspoon ground ginger
- Salt and pepper to taste
- Fresh cilantro leaves (for garnish)

Instructions:

1. Preheat your air fryer to 375°F (190°C).
2. In an air fryer-safe skillet, heat the olive oil over medium heat. Add the finely diced onion and cook for about 3 minutes, or until it becomes translucent.
3. Stir in the minced garlic, ground cumin, ground coriander, ground cinnamon, and ground ginger. Cook for an extra 1-2 minutes until the spices are fragrant.
4. Add the sliced carrots to the skillet and cook for 5-7 minutes, or until they start to soften.
5. Pour in the low-sodium vegetable broth, canned diced tomatoes, drained and rinsed chickpeas, salt, and pepper. Stir to combine all the ingredients.
6. Transfer the skillet to the air fryer basket and cook for 25-30 minutes, or until the carrots are tender and the flavors have melded together. Stir occasionally to prevent sticking.
7. Once the Moroccan Chickpea and Carrot Tagine is ready, garnish with fresh cilantro leaves.

Nutritional Information (per serving):

- Carbs: 41g
- Fats: 8g
- Fiber: 12g
- Protein: 9g

Spanish White Bean and Kale Salad with Sherry Vinaigrette

Prep Time: 15 minutes
Cook Time: 0 minutes
Number of Servings: 4

Ingredients:

For the Salad:

- 4 cups fresh kale leaves, stems removed and leaves chopped
- 2 cans (15 oz each) white beans (cannellini or Great Northern), drained and rinsed
- 1 red onion, thinly sliced
- 1/4 cup sliced almonds, toasted
- 1/4 cup crumbled feta cheese (optional)

For the Sherry Vinaigrette:

- 1/4 cup olive oil
- 2 tablespoons sherry vinegar

- 1 teaspoon Dijon mustard
- 1 clove garlic, minced
- Salt and pepper to taste

Instructions:

For the Sherry Vinaigrette:

1. In a small bowl, whisk the olive oil, sherry vinegar, Dijon mustard, minced garlic, salt, and pepper until well combined. Set aside.

For the Salad:

1. Preheat your air fryer to 375°F (190°C).
2. In an air fryer-safe skillet, spread out the sliced almonds and toast them in the air fryer for about 2-3 minutes until they become golden brown. Keep a close eye on them to prevent burning. Once toasted, take them out from the air fryer and set aside to cool.
3. In a large bowl, add the chopped kale leaves, drained and rinsed white beans, and thinly sliced red onion.
4. Drizzle the prepared Sherry Vinaigrette over the salad ingredients.
5. Toss the salad to ensure the dressing is evenly distributed.
6. If using, sprinkle the toasted sliced almonds and crumbled feta cheese (optional) over the top of the salad.
7. Serve the Spanish White Bean and Kale Salad immediately as a refreshing and nutritious side dish.

Nutritional Information (per serving, without feta cheese):

- Carbs: 30g
- Fats: 16g
- Fiber: 7g
- Protein: 9g

Lebanese Mujadara with Lentils and Brown Rice

Prep Time: 15 minutes
Cook Time: 40 minutes
Number of Servings: 4

Ingredients:

- 1 cup brown rice
- 1 cup dried brown or green lentils
- 2 large onions, thinly sliced
- 4 cups water
- 2 tablespoons olive oil
- 1 teaspoon ground cumin
- 1 teaspoon ground coriander
- Salt and pepper to taste
- Fresh parsley leaves (for garnish)

Instructions:

1. Preheat your air fryer to 375°F (190°C).

2. In an air fryer-safe skillet, heat one tablespoon of olive oil over medium heat. Add the thinly sliced onions and cook for about 20-25 minutes, stirring occasionally, until they become deeply caramelized and crispy. Take out the caramelized onions from the skillet and set them aside.

3. In the same skillet, add the remaining one tablespoon of olive oil. Stir in the ground cumin and ground coriander and cook for about 1-2 minutes until the spices are fragrant.

4. Add the brown rice and dried lentils to the skillet, stirring to coat them with the spices.

5. Transfer the skillet to the air fryer basket and pour in the 4 cups of water. Cook for 30-35 minutes at 375°F (190°C), or until both the rice and lentils are tender and the liquid is absorbed. Stir occasionally to prevent sticking.

6. Season the Mujadara with salt and pepper to taste.

7. Serve the Lebanese Mujadara hot, garnished with the caramelized onions and fresh parsley leaves.

Nutritional Information (per serving):

- Carbs: 63g
- Fats: 7g
- Fiber: 15g
- Protein: 16g

DESSERTS

Orange and Almond Flourless Cake

Prep Time: 15 minutes **Cook Time:** 30 minutes **Number of Servings:** 8

Ingredients:

- 2 large oranges
- 6 eggs
- 1 cup almond meal
- 1/2 cup honey
- 1 teaspoon baking powder
- 1/2 teaspoon vanilla extract

Instructions:

1. Wash the oranges thoroughly, then place them in a pot of water and bring to a boil. Simmer for 1 hour until the oranges are soft. Drain and let them cool.
2. Preheat your air fryer to 320°F (160°C).
3. Cut the cooled oranges into quarters, remove any seeds, and then blend them until you have a smooth orange puree.
4. In a mixing bowl, beat the eggs and add the almond meal, honey, baking powder, and vanilla extract. Mix until well combined.
5. Add the orange puree to the mixture and stir until it's fully incorporated.
6. Grease a cake pan suitable for your air fryer and pour the batter into it.
7. Place the cake pan in the air fryer basket and cook at 320°F (160°C) for 30 minutes. You may need to adjust the time slightly based on your air fryer's performance; the cake should be firm to the touch and a toothpick inserted into the center should come out clean.
8. Once done, carefully take out the cake from the air fryer and let it cool in the pan for 10 minutes before transferring it to a wire rack to cool completely.

Nutritional Information (per serving):

- Carbs: 23g
- Fats: 9g
- Fiber: 3g
- Protein: 6g

Greek Baklava Cheesecake

Prep Time: 20 minutes **Cook Time:** 30 minutes **Number of Servings:** 8

Ingredients:

- 1 cup crushed walnuts
- 1/4 cup honey
- 1/2 teaspoon ground cinnamon
- 1/4 cup melted unsalted butter
- 2 cups low-fat Greek yogurt
- 2 eggs
- 1/4 cup granulated sugar
- 1 teaspoon vanilla extract
- 1/4 cup whole wheat flour
- 8 sheets phyllo dough, thawed
- Cooking spray (for greasing)

Instructions:

1. In a bowl, add the crushed walnuts, honey, and ground cinnamon. Set this honey-walnut mixture aside.
2. In another bowl, whisk the Greek yogurt, eggs, granulated sugar, and vanilla extract until well blended. Gradually add the whole wheat flour and mix until the batter is smooth.
3. Preheat your air fryer to 350°F (175°C).
4. Take one sheet of phyllo dough and brush it lightly with melted unsalted butter. Place it in the bottom of a greased 8-inch round cake pan. Repeat this process with four more sheets, layering them and rotating each sheet slightly for even coverage.
5. Spread half of the honey-walnut mixture evenly over the phyllo dough layers.
6. Pour the Greek yogurt batter over the honey-walnut layer.
7. Layer the remaining three sheets of phyllo dough, brushing each with melted butter as before. Make sure to rotate and overlap the sheets for even coverage.
8. Spread the remaining honey-walnut mixture over the top phyllo layer.
9. Place the cake pan in the air fryer basket and cook at 350°F (175°C) for about 30 minutes or until the cheesecake is set and the top is golden brown. Check for doneness by inserting a toothpick into the center; it should come out clean when the cheesecake is done.
10. Once done, carefully take out the Baklava Cheesecake from the air fryer and let it cool in the pan for 15 minutes. Then, transfer it to the refrigerator and chill for at least 2 hours before serving.

Nutritional Information (per serving):

- Carbs: 27g
- Fats: 14g

- Fiber: 2g
- Protein: 8g

Honey and Pistachio Semolina Cake

Prep Time: 20 minutes **Cook Time:** 30 minutes **Number of Servings:** 8

Ingredients:

- 1 cup fine semolina
- 1/2 cup plain Greek yogurt
- 1/2 cup honey
- 1/4 cup olive oil
- 1/4 cup crushed pistachios
- 1 teaspoon baking powder
- 1/2 teaspoon vanilla extract
- Zest of 1 lemon
- Zest of 1 orange

For the Syrup:

- 1/2 cup honey
- 1/2 cup water
- Juice of 1 lemon
- Juice of 1 orange

Instructions:

1. In a mixing bowl, add the fine semolina, plain Greek yogurt, honey, olive oil, crushed pistachios, baking powder, vanilla extract, lemon zest, and orange zest. Mix until all ingredients are well combined.
2. Preheat your air fryer to 350°F (175°C).
3. Grease a round cake pan that fits inside your air fryer.
4. Pour the semolina cake batter into the greased cake pan and spread it out evenly.
5. Place the cake pan in the air fryer basket and cook at 350°F (175°C) for approximately 30 minutes or until the cake is golden brown on top and a toothpick inserted into the center comes out clean.
6. While the cake is cooking, prepare the syrup. In a small saucepan, add 1/2 cup of honey, 1/2 cup of water, lemon juice, and orange juice. Bring to a boil, then reduce the heat and simmer for about 5 minutes, allowing the syrup to thicken slightly.
7. Once the cake is done, remove it from the air fryer and immediately pour the hot syrup over the hot cake. Allow the cake to absorb the syrup for at least 15 minutes.
8. Slice the cake into 8 servings and serve warm or at room temperature.

Nutritional Information (per serving):

- Carbs: 47g
- Fats: 12g
- Fiber: 2g

- Protein: 4g

Date and Walnut Stuffed Figs

Prep Time: 15 minutes **Cook Time:** 8 minutes **Number of Servings:** 4

Ingredients:

- 8 large dried figs
- 8 walnut halves
- 4 Medjool dates, pitted
- 1 teaspoon olive oil
- 1/2 teaspoon ground cinnamon

Instructions:

1. Start by preparing the figs. Using a knife, make a vertical slit in each dried fig, about 3/4 of the way down, creating a pocket for the stuffing.
2. Take the pitted Medjool dates and cut each one in half lengthwise. Stuff one date half and one walnut half into each dried fig, ensuring they fit snugly.
3. Preheat your air fryer to 350°F (175°C).
4. Lightly brush the stuffed figs with olive oil to prevent them from drying out during cooking.
5. Place the stuffed figs in the air fryer basket in a single layer, ensuring not touching each other.
6. Sprinkle the ground cinnamon evenly over the stuffed figs.
7. Cook the figs in the air fryer at 350°F (175°C) for approximately 8 minutes or until they become slightly caramelized and tender.
8. Carefully take out the stuffed figs from the air fryer and let them cool for a few minutes before serving.

Nutritional Information (per serving):

- Carbs: 31g
- Fats: 6g
- Fiber: 5g
- Protein: 2g

Lemon Yogurt Parfait with Berries and Mint

Prep Time: 10 minutes **Cook Time:** 0 minutes **Number of Servings:** 2

Ingredients:

- 1 cup low-fat Greek yogurt
- Zest of 1 lemon
- 1 tablespoon lemon juice
- 1 tablespoon honey
- 1 cup mixed berries (e.g., strawberries, blueberries, raspberries)

- 2 tablespoons chopped fresh mint leaves

Instructions:

1. In a bowl, add the low-fat Greek yogurt, lemon zest, lemon juice, and honey. Mix sufficiently until the ingredients are thoroughly incorporated.

2. Preheat your air fryer to 350°F (175°C) for just a couple of minutes to slightly warm the parfait, if desired.

3. To assemble the parfait, take two serving glasses or bowls. Begin by adding a spoonful of the lemon yogurt mixture into the bottom of each glass.

4. Add a layer of mixed berries on top of the yogurt.

5. Continue layering with more lemon yogurt and berries until the glasses are filled, finishing with a dollop of yogurt on the top.

6. Sprinkle the chopped fresh mint leaves over the parfaits as a garnish.

7. If you'd like to slightly warm the parfait, place the glasses in the preheated air fryer for 1-2 minutes.

8. Serve the Lemon Yogurt Parfait with Berries and Mint immediately or refrigerate until ready to enjoy.

Nutritional Information (per serving):

- Carbs: 32g
- Fats: 1g
- Fiber: 4g
- Protein: 13g

Pistachio and Olive Oil Cake with Orange Glaze

Prep Time: 20 minutes **Cook Time:** 30 minutes **Number of Servings:** 8

Ingredients:

- 1 cup shelled pistachios
- 1 cup whole wheat flour
- 1 1/2 teaspoons baking powder
- 1/4 teaspoon salt
- 1/2 cup olive oil
- 3/4 cup granulated sugar
- 3 large eggs
- 1 teaspoon vanilla extract
- Zest of 1 orange
- Juice of 1 orange
- 1/2 cup powdered sugar (for the glaze)
- 1-2 tablespoons water (for the glaze)

Instructions:

1. Preheat your air fryer to 350°F (175°C).

2. In a food processor, finely grind the shelled pistachios

until they resemble a coarse flour. Be careful not to over-process, or they may turn into a paste.

3. In a mixing bowl, add the ground pistachios, whole wheat flour, baking powder, and salt. Mix sufficiently and set aside.

4. In another mixing bowl, whisk the olive oil and granulated sugar until well combined.

5. Add the eggs, one at a time, to the olive oil and sugar mixture, beating well after each addition.

6. Stir in the vanilla extract, orange zest, and orange juice.

7. Gradually add the dry ingredient mixture to the wet ingredients, mixing until just combined.

8. Grease a cake pan that fits inside your air fryer. Pour the cake batter into the pan, spreading it out evenly.

9. Place the cake pan in the air fryer basket and cook at 350°F (175°C) for approximately 30 minutes or until a toothpick inserted into the center of the cake comes out clean.

10. While the cake is cooking, prepare the orange glaze. In a small bowl, whisk the powdered sugar and water until you have a smooth glaze.

11. Once the cake is done, remove it from the air fryer and let it cool in the pan for 10 minutes before transferring it to a wire rack to cool completely.

12. Drizzle the orange glaze over the cooled cake.

Nutritional Information (per serving):

- Carbs: 45g
- Fats: 22g
- Fiber: 3g
- Protein: 6g

Greek Yogurt and Berry Popsicles

Prep Time: 10 minutes **Cook Time:** 0 minutes (freezing time required) **Number of Servings:** 6 popsicles

Ingredients:

- 2 cups low-fat Greek yogurt
- 1 cup mixed berries (e.g., strawberries, blueberries, raspberries)
- 2 tablespoons honey
- 1/2 teaspoon vanilla extract
- 6 popsicle molds

Instructions:

1. In a mixing bowl, add the low-fat Greek yogurt, honey,

and vanilla extract. Mix sufficiently until the ingredients are thoroughly combined.

2. Wash and prepare the mixed berries. If using strawberries, take out the stems and slice them into smaller pieces.

3. Gently fold the mixed berries into the Greek yogurt mixture until evenly distributed.

4. Carefully pour the yogurt and berry mixture into the popsicle molds, dividing it equally among them.

5. Insert popsicle sticks into each mold.

6. Place the popsicle molds in the freezer and let them freeze for at least 4 hours or until the popsicles are completely set.

7. Once the popsicles are frozen solid, take them out from the molds by running the molds under warm water briefly to loosen them.

8. Serve the Greek Yogurt and Berry Popsicles immediately.

Nutritional Information (per serving/popsicle):

- Carbs: 13g
- Fats: 1g
- Fiber: 1g
- Protein: 6g

Almond Flour and Lemon Zest Biscotti

Prep Time: 20 minutes **Cook Time:** 15 minutes **Number of Servings:** Approximately 12 biscotti

Ingredients:

- 2 cups almond flour
- 1/2 cup granulated sugar
- 1/2 teaspoon baking powder
- 1/4 teaspoon salt
- Zest of 2 lemons
- 2 large eggs
- 1 teaspoon vanilla extract
- 1/2 cup sliced almonds

Instructions:

1. Preheat your air fryer to 300°F (150°C).

2. In a mixing bowl, add the almond flour, granulated sugar, baking powder, salt, and lemon zest. Mix these dry ingredients until well combined.

3. In a separate bowl, whisk the eggs and vanilla extract.

4. Pour the egg mixture into the dry ingredients and stir until a sticky dough forms.

5. Fold in the sliced almonds into the dough, ensuring evenly distributed.

6. Place a sheet of parchment paper on a baking sheet or in a suitable air fryer tray.

7. Transfer the biscotti dough onto the parchment paper and shape it into a log about 12 inches long and 3 inches wide. Ensure it's even and compact.

8. Carefully place the parchment paper with the dough into the preheated air fryer.

9. Air fry the biscotti at 300°F (150°C) for approximately 15 minutes, or until the edges start to turn golden brown.

10. Take out the biscotti log from the air fryer and let it cool for about 10 minutes.

11. Reduce the air fryer temperature to 250°F (120°C).

12. Once the biscotti has cooled slightly, use a sharp knife to slice it into 1-inch thick pieces.

13. Place the sliced biscotti back onto the parchment paper in a single layer.

14. Air fry the biscotti at 250°F (120°C) for an extra 10-12 minutes, flipping them halfway through, until crisp and golden brown.

15. Let the biscotti cool completely on a wire rack before serving.

Nutritional Information (per biscotti):

- Carbs: 10g
- Fats: 7g
- Fiber: 2g
- Protein: 3g

Cardamom and Honey Poached Pears

Prep Time: 15 minutes **Cook Time:** 20 minutes **Number of Servings:** 4

Ingredients:

- 4 ripe pears (such as Bosc or Anjou)
- 4 cups water
- 1 cup honey
- 4 green cardamom pods, crushed
- 1 cinnamon stick
- 4 cloves
- 1 teaspoon vanilla extract
- 1/4 cup sliced almonds (for garnish)
- Greek yogurt (for serving)

Instructions:

1. Start by peeling the pears, leaving the stems intact if possible. Cut a small slice from the bottom of each pear to help them stand upright.

2. In your air fryer basket, add the water, honey, crushed cardamom pods, cinnamon stick, cloves, and vanilla extract. Stir to mix sufficiently.

3. Carefully place the prepared pears into the liquid mixture in the air fryer basket.

4. Preheat your air fryer to 350°F (175°C).

5. Poach the pears in the air fryer at 350°F (175°C) for approximately 15-20 minutes or until they become tender but not mushy. The cooking time may vary depending on the ripeness of the pears and your air fryer model.

6. While the pears are poaching, toast the sliced almonds in a dry pan over medium heat until they turn golden brown. Set them aside.

7. Once the pears are done, carefully take them out from the air fryer and let them cool slightly.

8. Serve each poached pear with a drizzle of the poaching liquid, a sprinkle of toasted sliced almonds, and a dollop of Greek yogurt.

Nutritional Information (per serving, excluding yogurt):

- Carbs: 73g
- Fats: 1g
- Fiber: 7g
- Protein: 1g

Chocolate Avocado Mousse with Sea Salt

Prep Time: 10 minutes **Cook Time:** 0 minutes **Number of Servings:** 4

Ingredients:

- 2 ripe avocados, pitted and peeled
- 1/4 cup unsweetened cocoa powder
- 1/4 cup honey
- 1 teaspoon vanilla extract
- A pinch of sea salt
- Fresh berries (for garnish, optional)

Instructions:

1. In a food processor, add the ripe avocados, unsweetened cocoa powder, honey, vanilla extract, and a pinch of sea salt.

2. Process the mixture until it's smooth and creamy. You may need to stop and scrape down the sides of the food processor to ensure all ingredients are well incorporated.

3. Taste the mousse and adjust the sweetness by adding more honey if desired.

4. Preheat your air fryer to 350°F (175°C) for a couple of minutes.

5. Spoon the chocolate avocado mousse into serving glasses or bowls.

6. Place the serving glasses or bowls in the preheated air fryer. Do not cover them.

7. Air fry the mousse at 350°F (175°C) for about 2-3 minutes to slightly warm it, if desired. This step is optional but can enhance the flavor.

8. Take out the serving glasses or bowls from the air fryer and let the mousse cool for a few minutes.

9. Garnish the Chocolate Avocado Mousse with fresh berries, if desired.

10. Serve the mousse immediately, or refrigerate it until ready to enjoy.

Nutritional Information (per serving, excluding berries):

- Carbs: 20g
- Fats: 15g
- Fiber: 7g
- Protein: 3g

Orange Blossom Honey and Almond Tart

Prep Time: 15 minutes **Cook Time:** 15 minutes **Number of Servings:** 8

Ingredients:

- 1 sheet store-bought puff pastry (approximately 9 inches by 9 inches)
- 1/2 cup almond meal
- 1/4 cup orange blossom honey
- 1/4 cup unsalted butter, melted
- 1 teaspoon vanilla extract
- Zest of 1 orange
- Sliced almonds (for garnish, optional)

Instructions:

1. Start by preheating your air fryer to 375°F (190°C) for a couple of minutes.

2. Place the puff pastry sheet on a clean surface and roll it out slightly to fit your air fryer tray. Trim any excess if needed to ensure it fits.

3. Carefully transfer the rolled-out puff pastry to the air fryer tray lined with parchment paper.

4. In a mixing bowl, add the almond meal, orange blossom honey, melted unsalted butter, vanilla extract, and orange zest. Mix until you have a smooth almond filling.

5. Spread the almond filling evenly over the puff pastry,

leaving a small border around the edges.

6. If desired, sprinkle sliced almonds over the almond filling for added texture and flavor.

7. Place the air fryer tray with the tart into the preheated air fryer.

8. Air fry the tart at 375°F (190°C) for approximately 12-15 minutes or until the pastry is golden brown and the almond filling is set.

9. Carefully take out the tart from the air fryer and let it cool for a few minutes.

10. Slice the Orange Blossom Honey and Almond Tart into 8 servings.

11. Serve the tart warm or at room temperature.

Nutritional Information (per serving):

- Carbs: 25g
- Fats: 16g
- Fiber: 1g
- Protein: 3g

Greek Yogurt and Lemon Poppy Seed Muffins

Prep Time: 15 minutes **Cook Time:** 15 minutes **Number of Servings:** 12 muffins

Ingredients:

- 1 1/2 cups whole wheat flour
- 1/2 cup almond meal
- 1/2 cup granulated sugar
- 1 tablespoon poppy seeds
- 1 1/2 teaspoons baking powder
- 1/2 teaspoon baking soda
- 1/4 teaspoon salt
- 1 cup plain Greek yogurt
- 1/4 cup olive oil
- 2 large eggs
- Zest of 2 lemons
- Juice of 1 lemon
- 1 teaspoon vanilla extract

Instructions:

1. Preheat your air fryer to 350°F (175°C) for a couple of minutes.

2. In a mixing bowl, add the whole wheat flour, almond meal, granulated sugar, poppy seeds, baking powder, baking soda, and salt. Mix until the dry ingredients are well combined.

3. In a separate mixing bowl, whisk the plain Greek yogurt, olive oil, eggs, lemon zest, lemon juice, and vanilla extract until the wet ingredients are fully incorporated.

4. Pour the wet ingredients into the dry ingredient mixture

and stir until just combined. Be careful not to overmix; a few lumps are okay.

5. Line a muffin tin with paper liners or lightly grease it.

6. Fill each muffin cup with the batter, dividing it equally among the 12 cups.

7. Place the muffin tin into the preheated air fryer. You may need to cook the muffins in batches if they don't all fit at once.

8. Air fry the muffins at 350°F (175°C) for approximately 15 minutes or until a toothpick inserted into the center of a muffin comes out clean.

9. Carefully take out the muffins from the air fryer and let them cool on a wire rack.

10. Once the muffins have cooled, ready to enjoy.

Nutritional Information (per muffin):

- Carbs: 26g
- Fats: 7g
- Fiber: 3g
- Protein: 6g

Pistachio and Fig Energy Bites

Prep Time: 15 minutes **Cook Time:** 0 minutes **Number of Servings:** Approximately 12 bites

Ingredients:

- 1 cup dried figs, stems removed
- 1/2 cup unsalted pistachios
- 1/4 cup rolled oats
- 1 tablespoon honey
- 1/2 teaspoon ground cinnamon
- A pinch of salt
- 1/4 cup shredded coconut (for coating, optional)

Instructions:

1. Start by preheating your air fryer to 350°F (175°C) for a couple of minutes.

2. In a food processor, add the dried figs, unsalted pistachios, rolled oats, honey, ground cinnamon, and a pinch of salt.

3. Process the mixture until it forms a sticky and well-combined dough. You may need to stop and scrape down the sides of the food processor as needed.

4. Once the mixture reaches a dough-like consistency, remove it from the food processor.

5. Take small portions of the dough and roll it between your hands to form bite-sized energy balls. Repeat until you've used all the dough.

6. If desired, roll each energy bite in shredded coconut to coat the exterior.

7. Place the energy bites on a plate or tray and refrigerate them for at least 30 minutes to help them set.

8. After chilling, the Pistachio and Fig Energy Bites are ready to be enjoyed.

Nutritional Information (per bite, without coconut coating):

- Carbs: 15g
- Fats: 3g
- Fiber: 2g
- Protein: 1g

Olive Oil and Citrus Semolina Cake

Prep Time: 20 minutes **Cook Time:** 20 minutes **Number of Servings:** 8

Ingredients:

- 1 cup fine semolina
- 1/2 cup granulated sugar
- 1/2 cup olive oil
- 2 large eggs
- Zest of 1 lemon
- Zest of 1 orange
- 1/4 cup fresh orange juice
- 1/4 cup fresh lemon juice
- 1 teaspoon baking powder
- 1/2 teaspoon vanilla extract
- A pinch of salt
- Powdered sugar (for dusting, optional)

Instructions:

1. Preheat your air fryer to 350°F (175°C) for a couple of minutes.

2. In a mixing bowl, add the fine semolina, granulated sugar, and baking powder. Mix sufficiently.

3. In a separate bowl, whisk the olive oil, eggs, lemon zest, orange zest, fresh lemon juice, fresh orange juice, vanilla extract, and a pinch of salt.

4. Gradually pour the wet mixture into the dry mixture and stir until you have a smooth batter.

5. Grease a cake pan that fits inside your air fryer. Pour the batter into the greased pan.

6. Place the cake pan in the preheated air fryer.

7. Air fry the cake at 350°F (175°C) for approximately 20 minutes or until a toothpick inserted into the center of the cake comes out clean.

8. Carefully take out the cake from the air fryer and let it cool for a few minutes.

9. If desired, dust the Olive Oil and Citrus Semolina Cake with powdered sugar for a decorative touch.

10. Slice the cake into 8 servings.

Nutritional Information (per serving, without powdered sugar):

- Carbs: 30g
- Fats: 21g
- Fiber: 1g
- Protein: 4g

Dark Chocolate-Dipped Dried Fruits and Nuts

Prep Time: 10 minutes **Cook Time:** 5 minutes **Number of Servings:** Varies (approximately 20 pieces)

Ingredients:

- 1/2 cup mixed dried fruits (e.g., apricots, figs, dates)
- 1/2 cup mixed nuts (e.g., almonds, walnuts, pistachios)
- 4 ounces dark chocolate (70% cocoa or higher)
- 1 teaspoon coconut oil
- A pinch of sea salt (optional)

Instructions:

1. Preheat your air fryer to 250°F (120°C) for a couple of minutes.

2. While the air fryer is preheating, prepare a tray or plate with parchment paper to place the dipped fruits and nuts on after dipping.

3. In a mixing bowl, add the mixed dried fruits and mixed nuts. You can chop the fruits and nuts into smaller pieces if desired.

4. Break the dark chocolate into smaller chunks and place them in a microwave-safe bowl. Add the coconut oil to the chocolate.

5. Microwave the chocolate and coconut oil in 15-20 second intervals, stirring each time, until the chocolate is completely melted and smooth. Be careful not to overheat the chocolate.

6. If desired, sprinkle a pinch of sea salt into the melted chocolate and stir to combine. This step is optional but can enhance the flavor.

7. Using a fork or a chocolate dipping tool, dip each piece of dried fruit and nut into the melted dark chocolate, ensuring well-coated.

8. Place the chocolate-dipped fruits and nuts onto the prepared parchment paper-lined tray or plate.

9. Once you've dipped all the fruits and nuts, place the tray in the preheated air fryer.

10. Air fry the chocolate-dipped fruits and nuts at 250°F (120°C) for about 5 minutes or until the chocolate is set. Keep a close eye on them to prevent burning.

11. Take out the tray from the air fryer and let the chocolate set completely at room temperature.

12. Once the chocolate is fully set, the Dark Chocolate-Dipped Dried Fruits and Nuts are ready to enjoy.

Nutritional Information (per piece, approximate):

- Carbs: 6g
- Fats: 5g
- Fiber: 1g
- Protein: 1g

Italian Olive Oil and Citrus Cake

Prep Time: 20 minutes **Cook Time:** 20 minutes **Number of Servings:** 8

Ingredients:

- 1 1/2 cups whole wheat flour
- 1/2 cup granulated sugar
- 1/2 cup olive oil
- 2 large eggs
- Zest of 1 lemon
- Zest of 1 orange
- 1/4 cup fresh orange juice
- 1/4 cup fresh lemon juice
- 1 teaspoon baking powder
- 1/2 teaspoon vanilla extract
- A pinch of salt
- Powdered sugar (for dusting, optional)

Instructions:

1. Preheat your air fryer to 350°F (175°C) for a couple of minutes.

2. In a mixing bowl, add the whole wheat flour, granulated sugar, baking powder, and a pinch of salt. Mix sufficiently.

3. In a separate mixing bowl, whisk the olive oil, eggs, lemon zest, orange zest, fresh lemon juice, fresh orange juice, and vanilla extract until the wet ingredients are fully incorporated.

4. Gradually pour the wet mixture into the dry mixture and stir until just combined. Be careful not to overmix; a few lumps are okay.

5. Grease a cake pan that fits inside your air fryer. Pour the batter into the greased pan.

6. Place the cake pan in the preheated air fryer.

7. Air fry the cake at 350°F (175°C) for approximately 20 minutes or until a toothpick

inserted into the center of the cake comes out clean.

8. Carefully take out the cake from the air fryer and let it cool for a few minutes.

9. If desired, dust the Italian Olive Oil and Citrus Cake with powdered sugar for a decorative touch.

10. Slice the cake into 8 servings.

Nutritional Information (per serving, without powdered sugar):

- Carbs: 25g
- Fats: 16g
- Fiber: 1g
- Protein: 4g

Mediterranean Chia Seed Pudding with Pomegranate

Prep Time: 5 minutes (plus overnight chilling) **Cook Time:** 0 minutes **Number of Servings:** 2

Ingredients:

- 1/4 cup chia seeds
- 1 cup unsweetened almond milk
- 1/2 teaspoon pure honey
- 1/4 teaspoon ground cinnamon
- 1/4 teaspoon pure vanilla extract
- 1/4 cup pomegranate seeds
- 1 tablespoon sliced almonds
- Fresh mint leaves (for garnish, optional)

Instructions:

1. In a bowl, add the chia seeds and unsweetened almond milk. Mix sufficiently to ensure the chia seeds are fully submerged in the milk.

2. Add the pure honey, ground cinnamon, and pure vanilla extract to the chia seed mixture. Stir until all the ingredients are well combined.

3. Cover the bowl with plastic wrap or a lid and refrigerate it overnight or for at least 4 hours. This allows the chia seeds to absorb the liquid and create a pudding-like consistency.

4. Before serving, give the chia seed pudding a good stir to evenly distribute the ingredients.

5. Divide the pudding into two serving glasses or bowls.

6. Top each serving with pomegranate seeds and sliced almonds.

7. If desired, garnish with fresh mint leaves for an extra pop of flavor and color.

8. Serve the Mediterranean Chia Seed Pudding with Pomegranate immediately or refrigerate for a few more

hours if you prefer it extra cold.

Nutritional Information (per serving):

- Carbs: 20g
- Fats: 9g
- Fiber: 10g
- Protein: 6g

Pistachio and Apricot Protein Balls

Prep Time: 15 minutes **Cook Time:** 0 minutes **Number of Servings:** Approximately 12 balls

Ingredients:

- 1 cup dried apricots
- 1 cup unsalted pistachios
- 1/4 cup rolled oats
- 2 tablespoons honey
- 2 tablespoons vanilla protein powder
- 1/2 teaspoon ground cinnamon
- A pinch of salt
- Shredded coconut (for rolling, optional)

Instructions:

1. Start by preheating your air fryer to 250°F (120°C) for a couple of minutes.
2. In a food processor, add the dried apricots, unsalted pistachios, rolled oats, honey, vanilla protein powder, ground cinnamon, and a pinch of salt.
3. Process the mixture until it forms a sticky and well-combined dough. You may need to stop and scrape down the sides of the food processor as needed.
4. Once the mixture reaches a dough-like consistency, remove it from the food processor.
5. Take small portions of the dough and roll it between your hands to form bite-sized protein balls. Repeat until you've used all the dough.
6. If desired, roll each protein ball in shredded coconut to coat the exterior.
7. Place the protein balls on a plate or tray and refrigerate them for at least 30 minutes to help them set.
8. After chilling, the Pistachio and Apricot Protein Balls are ready to be enjoyed.

Nutritional Information (per ball, without coconut coating):

- Carbs: 13g
- Fats: 5g
- Fiber: 2g
- Protein: 3g

Moroccan Orange Blossom Water Sorbet

Prep Time: 10 minutes **Cook Time:** 0 minutes **Number of Servings:** 4

Ingredients:

- 2 cups fresh orange juice (about 4-6 large oranges)
- 1/2 cup water
- 1/2 cup granulated sugar
- 1 tablespoon orange blossom water
- Zest of 1 orange
- Orange slices and mint leaves (for garnish, optional)

Instructions:

1. In a saucepan, add the water and granulated sugar. Heat the mixture over low heat, stirring constantly until the sugar completely dissolves. This will create a simple syrup.
2. Once the sugar is dissolved, take out the saucepan from heat and let the simple syrup cool to room temperature.
3. While the simple syrup is cooling, zest one orange to get the zest.
4. Squeeze the oranges to extract two cups of fresh orange juice.
5. In a mixing bowl, add the fresh orange juice, orange zest, and orange blossom water.
6. Once the simple syrup has cooled, add it to the orange juice mixture and stir sufficiently to combine.
7. Pour the mixture into an ice cream maker or your air fryer's air frying basket.
8. If using an air fryer, set it to the lowest temperature setting (usually around 120°F or 50°C) and let it run for about 20 minutes to start the freezing process. If using an ice cream maker, follow the manufacturer's instructions.
9. After the initial freezing, transfer the mixture to a freezer-safe container and freeze for an extra 3-4 hours or until it reaches the desired sorbet consistency. Stir the sorbet every 30 minutes during this time to prevent ice crystals from forming.
10. Once the Moroccan Orange Blossom Water Sorbet has reached the right consistency, scoop it into serving bowls or glasses.
11. Garnish with orange slices and mint leaves if desired.

Nutritional Information (per serving, without garnish):

- Carbs: 43g
- Fats: 0g
- Fiber: 1g
- Protein: 0g

Chapter 10

30-Day Meal Plan

Here's a 30-day meal plan consisting of breakfast, lunch, and dinner using the recipes available in this cookbook. Just a reminder that you can adjust portion sizes and ingredients depending on your diet and preferences.

Week 1
Day 1:

- Breakfast: Greek Yogurt and Berry Popsicles
- Lunch: Mediterranean Watercress Salad with Pomegranate and Pistachios
- Dinner: Moroccan Spiced Grilled Swordfish with Saffron-infused Moroccan Couscous

Day 2:

- Breakfast: Lemon Yogurt Parfait with Berries and Mint
- Lunch: Greek Quinoa Salad with Feta and Kalamata Olives
- Dinner: Moroccan Chickpea and Vegetable Tagine

Day 3:

- Breakfast: Greek Lemon Orzo Soup with Spinach and Chicken
- Lunch: Italian Caprese Salad with Avocado and Balsamic Glaze
- Dinner: Tuscan Ribollita Soup with Kale

Day 4:

- Breakfast: Mediterranean Chia Seed Pudding with Pomegranate
- Lunch: Roasted Beet and Quinoa Salad with Citrus Dressing
- Dinner: Greek Lemon Garlic Chicken with Green Beans

Day 5:

- Breakfast: Spinach and Feta Stuffed Pasta Shells with Marinara
- Lunch: Mediterranean Cucumber Ribbon Salad with Dill Yogurt Dressing
- Dinner: Italian Stuffed Calamari with Spinach and Pine Nuts

Day 6:

- Breakfast: Greek-style Orzo Risotto with Sundried Tomatoes
- Lunch: Spanish Gazpacho with Avocado Salsa
- Dinner: Moroccan Baked Fish with Preserved Lemon and Olives

Day 7:

- Breakfast: Lemon Rosemary Grilled Turkey Breast
- Lunch: Mediterranean Stuffed Bell Peppers with Quinoa and Chickpeas
- Dinner: Harissa Spiced Grilled Swordfish

Week 2

Day 8:

- Breakfast: Greek Vegan Spanakopita with Tofu and Spinach
- Lunch: Mediterranean Watermelon Radish and Mint Salad
- Dinner: Moroccan Spiced Chicken Tagine

Day 9:

- Breakfast: Lemon Garlic Spaghetti with Roasted Cherry Tomatoes
- Lunch: Moroccan Harira Soup with Quinoa
- Dinner: Greek Baked Red Snapper with Mediterranean Salsa

Day 10:

- Breakfast: Vegan Greek Spinach and Rice Stuffed Tomatoes
- Lunch: Mediterranean Tuna and White Bean Salad

- Dinner: Spanish Baked Hake with Tomato and Bell Pepper Sauce

Day 11:
- Breakfast: Mediterranean Farro Risotto with Roasted Tomatoes
- Lunch: Chickpea and Artichoke Tagine
- Dinner: Lemon Dill Baked Salmon with Asparagus

Day 12:
- Breakfast: Moroccan Couscous Pilaf with Apricots and Almonds
- Lunch: Italian Caprese Salad with Avocado and Balsamic Glaze
- Dinner: Mediterranean Lentil and Spinach Soup

Day 13:
- Breakfast: Lemon Artichoke Linguine with Arugula and Walnuts
- Lunch: Mediterranean Watercress Salad with Pomegranate and Pistachios
- Dinner: Greek-style Stuffed Calamari

Day 14:
- Breakfast: Greek Baklava Cheesecake
- Lunch: Tabbouleh Salad with Cauliflower Rice
- Dinner: Moroccan Spiced Scallops with Roasted Red Pepper Sauce

Week 3

Day 15:
- Breakfast: Orange Blossom Honey and Almond Tart
- Lunch: Grilled Artichoke and Asparagus Salad with Lemon Herb Vinaigrette
- Dinner: Greek Lemon Garlic Chicken with Green Beans

Day 16:
- Breakfast: Greek Tzatziki Pasta Salad with Cucumber and Dill

- Lunch: Moroccan Red Lentil and Spinach Soup
- Dinner: Harissa Shrimp and Zucchini Noodles

Day 17:
- Breakfast: Lemon Rosemary Chicken and Quinoa Bowls
- Lunch: Roasted Fennel and Orange Salad with Toasted Hazelnuts
- Dinner: Mediterranean Stuffed Acorn Squash with Bulgur

Day 18:
- Breakfast: Italian Olive Oil and Citrus Cake
- Lunch: Mediterranean Lentil and Swiss Chard Soup
- Dinner: Lemon Herb Stuffed Trout with Almonds

Day 19:
- Breakfast: Lemon Garlic Turkey and Vegetable Skewers
- Lunch: Greek Tuna and White Bean Salad with Dill
- Dinner: Moroccan Spiced Chickpea and Spinach Saute

Day 20:
- Breakfast: Greek-style Butter Beans with Tomato and Dill
- Lunch: Radicchio and Blood Orange Salad with Toasted Pine Nuts
- Dinner: Moroccan Baked Fish with Preserved Lemon and Olives

Day 21:
- Breakfast: Almond Flour and Lemon Zest Biscotti
- Lunch: Mediterranean Roasted Veggie Tacos with Tahini Sauce
- Dinner: Harissa Spiced Grilled Swordfish

Week 4
Day 22:
- Breakfast: Mediterranean Chia Seed Pudding with Pomegranate

- Lunch: Italian Herbed Turkey Meatloaf with Roasted Vegetables
- Dinner: Moroccan Chickpea and Carrot Tagine

Day 23:
- Breakfast: Greek Lemon Garlic Turkey Cutlets with Tzatziki
- Lunch: Mediterranean Watermelon Radish and Mint Salad
- Dinner: Spanish Baked Hake with Tomato and Bell Pepper Sauce

Day 24:
- Breakfast: Lemon Garlic Spaghetti with Roasted Cherry Tomatoes
- Lunch: Mediterranean Cucumber Ribbon Salad with Dill Yogurt Dressing
- Dinner: Moroccan Spiced Chicken Tagine

Day 25:
- Breakfast: Greek-style Orzo Risotto with Sundried Tomatoes
- Lunch: Spanish Gazpacho with Avocado Salsa
- Dinner: Grilled Swordfish with Italian Salsa Verde

Day 26:
- Breakfast: Lemon Rosemary Grilled Turkey Breast
- Lunch: Mediterranean Stuffed Bell Peppers with Quinoa and Chickpeas
- Dinner: Moroccan Baked Fish with Preserved Lemon and Olives

Day 27:
- Breakfast: Greek Vegan Spanakopita with Tofu and Spinach
- Lunch: Mediterranean Watercress Salad with Pomegranate and Pistachios
- Dinner: Moroccan Spiced Chicken Tagine

Day 28:

- Breakfast: Lemon Garlic Spaghetti with Roasted Cherry Tomatoes
- Lunch: Moroccan Harira Soup with Quinoa
- Dinner: Greek Baked Red Snapper with Mediterranean Salsa

Day 29:

- Breakfast: Mediterranean Farro Risotto with Roasted Tomatoes
- Lunch: Chickpea and Artichoke Tagine
- Dinner: Lemon Dill Baked Salmon with Asparagus

Day 30:

- Breakfast: Moroccan Couscous Pilaf with Apricots and Almonds
- Lunch: Italian Caprese Salad with Avocado and Balsamic Glaze
- Dinner: Moroccan Spiced Scallops with Roasted Red Pepper Sauce

Conclusion

As you near the end of the Mediterranean Air Fryer Cookbook, take a moment to appreciate the delightful and nutritious journey you have embarked on. This chapter concludes your experience, offering a satisfying ending to your exploration of Mediterranean flavors using the air fryer.

Enjoying Your New-Found Mediterranean Lifestyle with Your Air Fryer

Imagine sitting at a table with a view of the sparkling Mediterranean Sea. The breeze carries the scent of olive groves and the sound of laughter from a lively market nearby. In this final section, we invite you to appreciate not only the dishes you've prepared but also the lifestyle that the Mediterranean diet represents.

You have learned to cook delicious Mediterranean recipes with your air fryer and have adopted a way of eating associated with improved health and longevity. The Mediterranean diet focuses on consuming fresh, whole foods, incorporating heart-healthy fats, and enjoying every bite. With the air fryer, you can recreate these traditions in your own kitchen.

By employing the traditional principles of Mediterranean cuisine and the modern convenience of the air fryer, you have found a perfect blend of tradition and innovation. This powerful duo allows you to enjoy delicious dishes that promote good health.

As you enjoy the final bites of your Mediterranean dish cooked in the air fryer, remember that this isn't just the conclusion of a cookbook but the start of a lifelong passion for delicious and nutritious cooking. Incorporate the Mediterranean lifestyle into your life, not just in your recipes, but also in your attitude towards food, health, and overall well-being. The air fryer can help you prepare vibrant and nutritious Mediterranean dishes whenever you want. Bon appétit!

Recipe Index

A

Almond Flour and Lemon Zest Biscotti 168

Artichoke and Sun-Dried Tomato Stuffed Peppers 103

Arugula and Roasted Grape Salad with Balsamic Vinaigrette 15

B

Baked Cod with Mediterranean Tomato Sauce 50

Baked Lemon Herb Haddock 51

C

Cardamom and Honey Poached Pears 169

Chickpea and Artichoke Tagine 146

Chickpea and Spinach Salad with Lemon-Tahini Dressing 15

Chocolate Avocado Mousse with Sea Salt 170

Cilantro and Lemon Couscous with Dried Fruits and Nuts 97

D

Dark Chocolate-Dipped Dried Fruits and Nuts 175

Date and Walnut Stuffed Figs 165

E

Eggplant and Lentil Moussaka 107

Eggplant and Zucchini Moussaka 92

G

Garlic and Herb Shrimp Skewers 49

Greek Avgolemono Soup with Shrimp 27

Greek Baked Red Snapper with Mediterranean Salsa 59

Greek Baklava Cheesecake 162

Greek Gigantes Plaki (Baked Giant Beans) 145

Greek Lemon Chickpea Soup 33

Greek Lemon Garlic Chicken with Green Beans 76

Greek Lemon Garlic Turkey Cutlets with Tzatziki 87

Greek Lemon Orzo Soup with Spinach and Chicken 44

Greek Lemon Rice Soup with Kale 38

Greek Lemon Rosemary Chicken Thighs 79

Greek Orzo and Tomato Pilaf 134

Greek Quinoa Salad with Feta and Kalamata Olives 6

Greek Spinach and Feta Stuffed Shells 117

Greek Stuffed Sole with Spinach and Feta 53

Greek Tuna and White Bean Salad with Dill 21

Greek Tzatziki Pasta Salad with Cucumber and Dill 127

Greek Vegan Spanakopita with Tofu and Spinach 112

Greek Yogurt and Berry Popsicles 167

Greek Yogurt and Lemon Poppy Seed Muffins 172

Greek-Style Black-Eyed Peas with Spinach and Tomatoes 157

Greek-Style Butter Beans with Tomato and Dill 150

Greek-Style Gigantes Beans with Tomato and Parsley 155

Greek-style Orzo Risotto with Sundried Tomatoes 138

Greek-style Seafood Paella 64

Greek-style Stuffed Calamari 50

Grilled Artichoke and Asparagus Salad with Lemon Herb Vinaigrette 18

Grilled Halloumi Salad with Fig Vinaigrette 9

Grilled Harissa Chicken Thighs 71

Grilled Swordfish with Italian Salsa Verde 61

H

Harissa Roasted Quail with Mint Yogurt Sauce 77

Harissa Shrimp and Zucchini Noodles 60

Harissa Spiced Chickpea and Spinach Saute 154

Harissa Spiced Grilled Swordfish 47

Harissa Spiced Lentil Tacos 149

Honey and Pistachio Semolina Cake 164

I

Italian Brown Rice Risotto with Wild Mushrooms 132

Italian Cannellini Bean and Escarole Soup 148

Italian Caprese Salad with Avocado and Balsamic Glaze 21

Italian Eggplant and Zucchini Ratatouille 111

Italian Farro and Roasted Vegetable Bowl 125

Italian Herb Roasted Turkey Cutlets 78

Italian Herbed Turkey Meatloaf with Roasted Vegetables 84

Italian Lentil and Mushroom Stuffed Bell Peppers 156

Italian Minestrone Soup with Cannellini Beans 41

Italian Olive Oil and Citrus Cake 176

Italian Stuffed Calamari with Spinach and Pine Nuts 58

Italian White Bean and Escarole Salad with Lemon-Dijon Dressing 151

Italian White Bean and Kale Soup with Turkey Sausage 34

Italian-Style Lentil Salad with Sun-Dried Tomatoes 144

L

Lebanese Lentil and Rice Pilaf 118

Lebanese Mujadara with Lentils and Brown Rice 160

Lebanese Mujadara with Quinoa 148

Lebanese Red Lentil and Spinach Soup 37

Lemon Artichoke Linguine with Arugula and Walnuts 137

Lemon Chicken Orzo Soup with Spinach 26

Lemon Dill Baked Salmon with Asparagus 56

Lemon Garlic Shrimp and Asparagus Orzo 123

Lemon Garlic Spaghetti with Roasted Cherry Tomatoes 129

Lemon Garlic Turkey and Vegetable Skewers 82

Lemon Herb Stuffed Trout with Almonds 63

Lemon Oregano Turkey Meatballs 69

Lemon Rosemary Chicken and Quinoa Bowls 85

Lemon Rosemary Grilled Turkey Breast 73

Lemon Yogurt Parfait with Berries and Mint 165

M

Mediterranean Chia Seed Pudding with Pomegranate 177

Mediterranean Chicken and Artichoke Skewers 74

Mediterranean Chicken Shawarma 68

Mediterranean Cucumber Ribbon Salad with Dill Yogurt Dressing 17

Mediterranean Farro Risotto with Roasted Tomatoes 120

MEDITERRANEAN AIR FRYER COOKBOOK FOR WEIGHT LOSS

Mediterranean Lentil and Eggplant Casserole 153

Mediterranean Lentil and Spinach Soup 31

Mediterranean Lentil and Swiss Chard Soup 42

Mediterranean Roasted Vegetable Platter 96

Mediterranean Roasted Veggie Tacos with Tahini Sauce 100

Mediterranean Spaghetti Squash with Roasted Red Pepper Sauce 141

Mediterranean Stuffed Acorn Squash with Bulgur 114

Mediterranean Stuffed Bell Peppers with Quinoa and Chickpeas 104

Mediterranean Tuna and White Bean Salad 8

Mediterranean Watercress Salad with Pomegranate and Pistachios 10

Mediterranean Watermelon Radish and Mint Salad 24

Moroccan Baked Fish with Preserved Lemon and Olives 48

Moroccan Chermoula Grilled Prawns 52

Moroccan Chicken and Olive Tagine 80

Moroccan Chicken with Apricots and Almonds 75

Moroccan Chickpea and Carrot Tagine 158

Moroccan Chickpea and Date Tagliatelle 124

Moroccan Chickpea and Eggplant Tagine 113

Moroccan Chickpea and Spinach Stew 40

Moroccan Chickpea and Vegetable Tagine 106

Moroccan Couscous Pilaf with Apricots and Almonds 140

Moroccan Harira Soup with Quinoa 45

Moroccan Orange Blossom Water Sorbet 179

Moroccan Spiced Cauliflower Salad with Tahini 22

Moroccan Spiced Chicken Skewers with Yogurt-Harissa Dip 88

Moroccan Spiced Chicken Tagine 70

Moroccan Spiced Couscous with Roasted Vegetables 131

Moroccan Spiced Scallops with Roasted Red Pepper Sauce 66

O

Olive Oil and Citrus Semolina Cake 174

Orange and Almond Flourless Cake 162

Orange Blossom Honey and Almond Tart 171

P

Pistachio and Apricot Protein Balls 178

Pistachio and Fig Energy Bites 173

Pistachio and Olive Oil Cake with Orange Glaze 166

R

Radicchio and Blood Orange Salad with Toasted Pine Nuts 14

Roasted Beet and Quinoa Salad with Citrus Dressing 11

Roasted Carrot and Chickpea Salad with Cumin-Lemon Dressing 19

Roasted Eggplant and Tomato Soup 32

Roasted Fennel and Orange Salad with Toasted Hazelnuts 16

Roasted Tomato and Basil Soup with White Beans 28

S

Saffron-infused Moroccan Couscous 121

Sardine and Olive Tapenade Stuffed Bell Peppers 54

Spanakopita Stuffed Portobello Mushrooms 99

Spanish Baked Hake with Tomato and Bell Pepper Sauce 62

Spanish Chickpea and Chorizo Stew 152

Spanish Chilled Almond and Garlic Soup (Ajo Blanco) 43

Spanish Gazpacho with Avocado Salsa 30

Spanish Grilled Mackerel with Romesco Sauce 57

Spanish White Bean and Chorizo Stew 143

Spanish White Bean and Garlic Soup 39

Spanish White Bean and Kale Salad with Sherry Vinaigrette 159

Spicy Moroccan Lentil Soup 25

Spinach and Chickpea Curry 94

Spinach and Feta Stuffed Chicken Breast 72

Spinach and Ricotta Stuffed Pasta Shells with Marinara 135

Spinach and Ricotta Stuffed Shells with Tomato Sauce 128

T

Tabbouleh Salad with Cauliflower Rice 12

Tomato and Basil Quinoa Soup 36

Tuscan Herb Stuffed Quail 83

Tuscan Ribollita Soup with Kale 29

Tuscan White Bean and Rosemary Hummus 147

Tuscan-style Clam and Cannellini Bean Stew 55

Tuscan-style Turkey and White Bean Soup 89

V

Vegan Eggplant Parmesan with Spaghetti Squash 98

Vegan Greek Spinach and Rice Stuffed Tomatoes 105

Vegan Italian Artichoke and Spinach Lasagna 109

Vegan Italian Pasta Primavera with Lemon Garlic Sauce 115

Vegan Mediterranean Stuffed Bell Peppers 93

Vegan Moroccan Lentil Stew 101

W

Watermelon and Mint Salad with Feta 7

Z

Zucchini Ribbon Salad with Basil Pesto 13

Printed in Great Britain
by Amazon